Cross-Cultural Explorations
Activities in Culture and Psychology

Susan Goldstein
University of Redlands

Allyn and Bacon
Boston   London   Toronto   Sydney   Tokyo   Singapore

About the Author

Susan B. Goldstein earned her Ph.D. from the University of Hawaii as a grantee from the East-West Center. She is currently an associate professor of psychology at the University of Redlands in southern California. Her research interests include stigma, cultural perspectives on the mediation of disputes, and intergroup relations. She has been teaching courses on culture and psychology for the past 15 years.

Copyright © 2000 by Allyn & Bacon
A Pearson Education Company
160 Gould Street
Needham Heights, Massachusetts 02494-2130

Internet: www.abacon.com

ISBN 0-205-28520-1

Printed in the United States of America

10 9 8 7 6 5 4 3 2 1   03 02 01 00 99

Table of Contents

Chapter 4. Culture and Developmental Processes

Chapter 5. Personality, Emotion, and the Self in Cultural Context

Chapter 6. Health, Stress, and Coping Across Cultures

Chapter 7. Culture and Social Behavior

Chapter 8. Intergroup Relations

Chapter 9. Intercultural Interaction

Preface

The Study of Culture and Psychology

Imagine that a visitor from another nation comes to your country to write a travel guide for his compatriots. He writes about various aspects of life that a traveler would need to understand, such as customs, food, transportation, and regulations. However, he gathers all of his information in one large city and never travels to other areas of the country. Would you feel you could rely on this guide were you to journey to areas outside of that city? In many ways this situation is analogous to research in the field of psychology. Most of the research findings included in psychology textbooks are derived from the study of a rather limited population, primarily white, middle-class college students from the United States, Canada, and Western Europe. Yet these findings are often presented as if they apply to the behavior of all humans throughout the world. Cross-cultural psychologists have produced data to challenge the notion that these research findings are universal (Smith & Bond, 1999, for example, discuss challenges to the universality of social psychological principles). Not only are many of these findings of questionable validity when applied outside of the regions where the research was conducted, they are of questionable validity when applied uniformly within those regions. This lack of applicability within the United States, Canada, and Western Europe is due to biases in psychological theory and research that result from the failure to acknowledge diversity associated with gender, race, social class (Denmark, 1994; Graham, 1992; Reid & Kelly, 1994), age (Schaie, 1988), sexual orientation (Herek, Kimmel, Amaro, & Melton, 1991) and disability (Fine & Asch, 1988). Thus, just as we may be misled by using the travel guide described above to negotiate through diverse regions of your country, we may also be misled by using "mainstream" psychological research to understand the diversity of human behavior.

Psychology as an academic discipline has only recently begun to recognize the importance of a cultural perspective. When I finished graduate school and began interviewing for college teaching positions nearly a decade ago, I found I often had to explain to potential employers what it meant to be trained in cross-cultural psychology (in fact, one department chair at a well-respected liberal arts college asked if my background prepared me to teach parapsychology -- the study of psychic phenomena!). While cultural perspectives remain somewhat marginalized in the field of psychology (Goldstein, 1995), they have clearly gained a more central role in recent years. More colleges and universities are offering courses in cross-cultural psychology or have revised courses in traditional areas of psychology so as to be more inclusive of a cultural perspective. Authors of textbooks across the psychology curriculum have made corresponding changes with greater focus on the role of culture in understanding human behavior. This book was designed to contribute to the inclusion of cultural perspectives in the psychology curriculum by providing students with hands-on experiences that facilitate the understanding and application of major concepts and principles in the study of culture and psychology.

Psychologists have taken a number of approaches to studying the impact of culture on human behavior. *Cross-cultural psychology* focuses on comparing specific behaviors across cultures. For example, Punamaki and Joustie (1998) studied the effect of a violent environment on dreams in a comparison of the dream content of Finnish and Palestinian children. Cross-cultural psychologists work within a wide variety of research areas including social, developmental, cognitive, clinical, and organizational psychology. Rather than being characterized by a distinct content area, cross-cultural psychology is identified by the unique methods used to make comparisons across cultures, methods that are used to strive toward identifying universal principles of human behavior.

The *indigenous psychologies* approach utilizes concepts and methods that arise from within the culture of interest (Kim & Berry, 1993). Because concepts that result from indigenous psychologies may be compared, indigenous psychology may also be considered a subdomain of cross-cultural psychology (Ho, 1998). Enriquez (1993), for example, has described a form of indigenous psychology in the Philippines called *liberation psychology,* which has arisen from the colonial history of that nation.

Cultural psychology focuses on detailing the interrelationships among forms of behavior within a specific culture and is generally less concerned with cross-cultural comparisons and the use of quantitative research methods. An example of this approach to culture and psychology might be the study of social ethnotheories in which interviews or open-ended questions are used to gather information about the human qualities valued by a specific group, such as in regard to child rearing (Greenfield, 1997).

Ethnic psychology is concerned with the use of culturally appropriate methods to understand the behavior and experiences of members of specific ethnic groups, a term that has been applied primarily to the psychologies of historically marginalized groups in North America. For example, William Cross (1991) has developed a model of *nigrescence*, or Black racial identity, which has been used to explore aspects of mental health and self-concept among African Americans.

Psychological anthropology involves anthropological studies that make explicit and systematic use of psychological methods and concepts (Bock, 1995). An example of this approach is the "Six Cultures Project" directed by John and Beatrice Whiting. In this classic series of studies, hypotheses about the factors affecting children's behavior were tested with data collected by pairs of investigators who made intensive observations of children in six small communities across the globe.

The majority of activities in this book are derived from the field of cross-cultural psychology, although research findings from indigenous psychology, cultural psychology, ethnic psychology, and psychological anthropology are also represented. I hope that as you progress through the activities in this book you will gain a better understanding of how each of these approaches has contributed to our knowledge of the impact of culture on human behavior.

The Content and Structure of This Book

The activities that compose this book revolve around case studies, self-administered scales, mini-experiments, and the collection of content-analytic, observational, and interview data. Background material is included for any concepts not commonly addressed in introductory texts.

In this book, I have chosen to use a broad conceptualization of culture, inclusive of groups identified on a variety of dimensions in addition to nationality or race/ethnicity. This expanded view of culture and psychology reflects current thinking among cross-cultural scholars and allows for a discussion of culture in a context more relevant to the lives of many student readers.

The book is organized in terms of nine chapters of 10 activities each, representing major content areas in research on culture and psychology:

- Chapter 1, The Concept of Culture, addresses the definition of culture and some basic dimensions on which cultures differ.
- Chapter 2, Culture and Psychological Research, explores major issues and techniques in the conduct of cross-cultural research.
- Chapter 3, Culture and Basic Processes, brings a cross-cultural perspective to the processes of cognition, memory, and language.
- Chapter 4, Culture and Developmental Processes, focuses on socialization in cultural context and cultural variation in developmental processes.
- Chapter 5, Personality, Emotion, and the Self in Cultural Context, addresses the impact of culture on the construal of self, the study of personality across cultures, and the cross-cultural relevance of Western personality theory.
- Chapter 6, Health, Stress, and Coping Across Cultures, deals with major issues in cross-cultural research on physical and mental well-being.
- Chapter 7, Culture and Social Behavior, explores major research findings in the areas of conflict resolution, work-related behavior, close interpersonal relationships, and attribution theory.
- Chapter 8, Intergroup Relations, explores the phenomena of prejudice, discrimination, stereotyping, and marginalization.
- Chapter 9, Intercultural Interaction, deals with research on intercultural communication, adjustment, and training.

You will also find an appendix at the end of the book that includes a variety of resources to assist you in exploring culture and psychology. These include professional associations, scholarly journals, anti-hate organizations, and Internet resources. I hope that this appendix will serve as a useful reference as you approach the activities in this book as well as for cross-cultural pursuits outside of this course.

Discussing Diversity
Although students often take courses dealing with issues of culture and psychology because they are interested in dispelling stereotypes, you may find it is difficult to discuss such issues without creating or reinforcing stereotypical notions. Bronstein and Quina (1988) stated that the risk of creating stereotypes is particularly high when people are labeled on the basis of a single dimension and placed in opposition to other labeled groups for the purpose of comparison. This is precisely the format in which cross-cultural findings are typically presented. There are several strategies that may reduce the likelihood of discussing cultural differences in terms of stereotypes. Perhaps the most important strategy is to stay aware of the diversity *within* any cultural group. Bronstein and Quina suggest carefully examining research results in order to more clearly understand that within-group variability is generally greater than between-groups variability. The diversity within groups can also be reinforced by clearly specifying characteristics of research participants. Betancourt and Lopez (1993), for example, noted that culture, race, and ethnicity are frequently confounded with socioeconomic variables. Cross-cultural research should thus be discussed in terms of the specific characteristics of the research participants (such as social class and gender), and efforts should be made not to generalize these findings to all members of that cultural group. Specifying the characteristics of research participants is also important when discussing research in terms of race or ethnicity. Studies of Taiwanese or Malaysian participants, for example, should not be generalized to describe "Asian behavior." Similarly, data collected from predominantly white, North American college populations do not provide an appropriate basis for conclusions about "Western values" or "American behavior."

An additional strategy for addressing the tendency to stereotype is to learn about the mechanics of stereotyping and cognitive aspects of the stereotyping process (see, for example, Hamilton, Stroessner, & Driscoll, 1994). By regarding stereotyping as a result of errors in information processing, it is possible to separate stereotyping from prejudice and enable participants in discussions to point out stereotypic comments without making personal attacks. Some of the activities in Chapter 8 will help you learn to examine the source of specific stereotypes, explore errors involved in attention, categorization, memory, and attributional processes, and seek information to disconfirm these stereotypes.

The language used to discuss cultural factors may unknowingly create stereotypes by setting ethnocentric standards of comparison. For example, Segall, Dasen, Berry, and Poortinga (1990) pointed out the ethnocentric nature of terms used to describe changes in social and political environments, such as *Westernization, civilization, modernization*, and *detribalization*. In addition, cross-cultural psychologists frequently use a *Western/Non-Western* classification in describing cultural differences in behavior. This dichotomy reinforces the notion that what is Western is central, and thus the standard of comparison, and that all other cultures are less significant and less distinctive. The terms *white/nonwhite* produce a similar bias in emphasis. When possible, it may be preferable to discuss cross-cultural findings in terms of the specific cultural groupings involved (such as European American and Japanese) or in terms of the relevant variables underlying the comparison (such as individualism versus collectivism).

Comparisons between objects or phenomena that serve the same function need not be described using separate terms. For example, Moore (1988) noted the unnecessary practice of referring to the homes of African people as *huts* and that the word *tribe*, although frequently used to refer to diverse peoples within African nations, is rarely used to refer to diverse peoples within European nations. It is useful to question whether our language contributes to describing relevant cross-cultural differences, or if it serves only an evaluative purpose. Some of the activities in Chapter 3 may be particularly useful in exploring the role of language in shaping our thoughts and emotions.

References
Betancourt, H., & Lopez, S. R. (1993). The study of culture, ethnicity, and race in American psychology. *American Psychologist, 48*, 629-637.

Bock, P. K., (1995). *Rethinking psychological anthropology: Continuity and change in the study of human action.* Prospect Heights, IL: Waveland Press.

Bronstein, P., & Quina, K. (1988). Perspectives on gender balance and cultural diversity in the teaching of psychology. In P. Bronstein & K. Quina (Eds.), *Teaching a psychology of people: Resources for gender and sociocultural awareness* (pp. 3-11). Washington, DC.: American Psychological Association.

Cross, W. (1991). *Shades of Black: Diversity in African-American identity.* Philadelphia: Temple University Press.

Denmark, F. (1994). Engendering psychology. *American Psychologist, 49*, 329-334.

Enriquez, V. G. (1993). Developing a Filipino psychology. In U. Kim & J. W. Berry (Eds.). *Indigenous psychologies: Research and experience in cultural context* (pp. 152-169). Newbury Park, CA: Sage.

Fine, M., & Asch, A. (1988). Disability beyond stigma: Social interaction, discrimination, and activism. *Journal of Social Issues, 44*, 3-21.

Goldstein, S. B. (1995). Cross-cultural psychology as a curriculum transformation resource. *Teaching of Psychology, 22*, 228-232.

Graham, S. (1992). Most of the subjects were white and middle class. *American Psychologist, 47*, 629-639.

Greenfield, P. M. (1997). Culture as process: Empirical methods for cultural psychology. In J. W. Berry, Y. H. Poortinga, & J. Pandey (Eds.). *Handbook of cross-cultural psychology, Vol 1. Theory and method.* (2nd ed., pp. 301-346). Boston: Allyn & Bacon.

Hamilton, D. L., Stroessner, S. J., & Driscoll, D. M. (1994). Social cognition and the study of stereotyping. In P. G. Devine, D. L. Hamilton, & T. M. Ostrom (Eds.), *Social cognition: Impact on social psychology* (pp. 291-321). New York: Academic Press.

Herek, G., Kimmel, D. L., Amaro, H., & Melton, G. B. (1991). Avoiding heterosexist bias in psychological research. *American Psychologist, 46*, 957-963.

Ho, D. Y. F. (1998). Indigenous psychologies: Asian perspectives. *Journal of Cross-Cultural Psychology, 29*, 88-103.

Kim, U., & Berry, J. W. (1993). *Indigenous psychologies: Research and experience in cultural context.* Newbury Park, CA: Sage.

Moore, R. S. (1988). Racist stereotyping in the English language. In P. S. Rothenberg (Ed.), *Racism and sexism: An integrated study* (3rd ed., pp. 376-386). New York: St. Martin's.

Punamaki, R.-L., & Joustie, M. (1998). The role of culture, violence, and personal factors affecting dream content. *Journal of Cross-Cultural Psychology, 29,* 320-342.

Reid, P. T., & Kelly, K. (1994). Research on women of color: From ignorance to awareness. *Psychology of Women Quarterly, 18,* 477-486.

Schaie, K. W. (1988). Ageism in psychological research. *American Psychologist, 43,* 179-183.

Segall, M. H., Dasen, P. R., Berry, J. W., & Poortinga, Y. H. (1990). *Human behavior in global perspective.* New York: Pergamon.

Smith, P. B., & Bond, M. H. (1999). *Social psychology across cultures* (2nd ed.). Boston: Allyn & Bacon.

To the Student

Since I began teaching Introductory Psychology and Cross-Cultural Psychology over a decade ago, I have enjoyed devising new ways to involve my students in the exploration of culture and psychology. The activities in this book are a result of these efforts. I hope that you will find these activities exciting and challenging, that they provide you with a new perspective on human behavior, and that they help you to understand the role of culture in your own experiences and behaviors. Please read the instructions included in each activity carefully. Some of the activities involve collecting data from others and have specific directions regarding ethical considerations, such as maintaining confidentiality. Many of the activities have been modified in response to the feedback I received from my own students over the years. I would very much appreciate hearing from you about your experiences with these activities as well. You will find my address below.

To the Instructor

I often hear psychology instructors commenting on the difficulty of creating active learning experiences exploring cultural perspectives in psychology. Unlike other areas of psychology, one cannot easily ask students to replicate cross-cultural studies. Instead, this activity book provides students with a cross-cultural perspective through exploring their own cultural background, interviewing others with specific cross-cultural experiences, making cross-cultural comparisons using a broad interpretation of culture, and reading about cultures different from their own in the materials included in specific activities.

This book is designed for use as a supplement for courses specifically focusing on culture and human behavior, such as a cross-cultural psychology course, as well as a means to integrate cultural perspectives into an introductory psychology course. The nine chapters represent the topics addressed in most cross-cultural psychology textbooks and correspond to the organization of most introductory psychology texts as well.

The large number of activities included in this book allows you to select those best suited to your course. Since the activities address thought-provoking issues and require that students engage in critical thinking, they may be assigned prior to class or during class to be used as the basis for class discussion. Several of the activities would be appropriate as small group projects. Students can either complete the activity as a group or bring the completed activity to class and work in a group to evaluate the pooled data. Since the activities are printed on tear-out pages, they may be easily collected by instructors as individual assignments. Each of the activities may be assigned independently and out of sequence.

The instructor's manual that accompanies this book provides detailed suggestions on how to tailor specific activities to fit your course. It includes ideas for using the activities with more advanced students and for expanding the writing component of activities to include techniques drawn from the literature on writing across the curriculum, such as free writing, journaling, and peer review. The instructor's manual also includes a variety of lecture and discussion ideas, and video, text, and Internet materials related to specific activities in this book. As in my message to the students, I invite you to contact me with any feedback about your experiences with the activities. I hope you will find this book to be a helpful tool in guiding students through an exploration of the impact of culture on human behavior.

Acknowledgments
I have many people to thank for their generous assistance with this book, including Allyn & Bacon editor, Carolyn Merrill, and editorial assistants, Lara Zeises and Amy Goldmacher. My thinking about these activities was guided by the helpful suggestions of my colleague, Cheryl Rickabaugh, the students of the University of Hawaii and the University of Redlands, and the reviewers: John Adamopoulos, Grand Valley State University; Karen L. Butler, Johnson C. Smith University; Susan E. Dutch, Westfield State College; G. William Hill, Kennesaw State University; James M. Jones, University of Delaware; Frank F. Montalvo, University of Texas -- San Antonio; Connie Schick, Bloomsburg University, Yvonne Wells, Suffolk University; and Evangeline Wheeler, Towson University. My thanks also go out to Sandi Richey, University of Redlands Interlibrary Loan Librarian, who worked miracles to obtain resources from across the globe. I would not have been able to complete this book without the unending patience and encouragement of my family, in particular my husband, Paul Hisada, who devoted many hours to the computer-related aspects of this project and took on more than his share of juggling work and family in order to create time for me to write. Finally, I am thankful to my wonderful daughters, Lauren and Rachel, who have helped me to understand the need for all of us to embark upon cross-cultural explorations.

Susan Goldstein
Department of Psychology, University of Redlands
1200 East Colton Avenue, P. O. Box 3080
Redlands, CA 92373   E-mail: goldstei@uor.edu

Chapter 1. The Concept of Culture

Name _____   Date _____

Activity 1.1
IS PSYCHOLOGY CULTURE BOUND?

Psychology as a discipline strives to identify and describe universal principles of behavior. However, most psychological research has focused on a very limited population from which to draw conclusions about humans in general. Unfortunately, many psychology textbooks discuss research findings as if they are universal, even in cases where cross-cultural studies indicate otherwise. This activity asks you to think about a number of concepts taken at random from introductory psychology textbooks and consider the universality of each.

Directions: Read the description of each of the psychological concepts below. Then indicate in the space provided after each concept whether you believe it applies to all cultures or believe it to be limited to specific cultural groups. Write a brief explanation of your response. When you are finished you can check your answers on page 373.

1. *Susceptibility to visual illusions* - Though the two lines in the Müller-Lyer illusion below are the same length, the second line with the reverse arrowheads looks longer.

2. *The serial-position effect (primacy and recency)* -- The first few items and the last few items in a list are remembered better than the items in the middle of the list.

3. *The independent self* -- Each of us has a "self" that includes the unique qualities that distinguish us from others.

4. *Secure attachment* -- Ainsworth and colleagues (1978) have delineated three types of attachment: secure, avoidant, and ambivalent. Secure attachment is viewed as ideal in terms of the development of basic trust and other mental health indices.

5. *Delusions and hallucinations* -- According to the DSM-IV, delusions and hallucinations are signs of mental illness, specifically schizophrenia.

6. *Fundamental attribution error* -- The tendency to underestimate the impact of the situation and overestimate the impact of dispositional (personality) factors in explaining the behavior of others.

7. *Social loafing* -- The tendency for people to exert less effort when working as a group than when individually accountable.

Reference:
    Ainsworth, M. D. S., Blehar, M. D., Waters, E., & Wall, S. (1978). *Patterns of attachment: A psychological study of the Strange Situation*. Hillsdale, NJ: Lawrence Erlbaum.

Name _____   Date _____

Activity 1.2
WHAT IS CULTURE?

The concept of culture is not an easy one to define. Even among those who study culture and human behavior there are a large number of definitions in use. Perhaps the most straightforward definition is that of Melville Herskovits (1948) who proposed that culture is the human-made part of the environment. Harry Triandis and colleagues (1972) further suggest that culture has both physical components (such as tools, buildings, and works of art) and subjective components (such as roles, values, and attitudes). Recently, the term *culture* has been used more broadly to refer to the common values, beliefs, and behaviors within groups who share a nationality, ethnic heritage, disability, sexual orientation, or socioeconomic class, as well as to those who share a corporate identity, occupation, sport, or college campus. This activity encourages you to explore the meaning of culture by applying several commonly cited criteria (see for example, Brislin, 1993; Rohner, 1984; Singer, 1998; and Triandis, Vassiliou, Vassiliou, Tanaka, & Shanmugam, 1972) to determine whether a specific group is, in fact, a culture.

Directions: Identify a group that you think of as having its own culture. First describe this group, then by answering the questions below, decide whether this group has the characteristics of a culture.

Group Name and Description:

1. Does the group hold shared perspectives, norms, values, or assumptions that direct the behavior of its members? Please give an example.

2. Is information important to this group handed down through generations (or cohorts) of its members? Please give an example.

3. Does this group have a common language, dialect, or set of terms? Please give an example.

4. Are the perspectives and practices of this group widely shared among its members? Please give an example.

5. Do group members react emotionally when the perspectives or practices of this group are not upheld? Please give an example.

Conclusions: Discuss your conclusions about whether the group you chose to examine is a culture.

References:

Brislin, R. (1993). *Understanding cultures influence on behavior*. Orlando, FL: Harcourt Brace Jovanovich.

Herskovits, M. J. (1948). *Man and his works: The science of cultural anthropology*. New York: Knopf.

Rohner, R. (1984). Toward a conception of culture for cross-cultural psychology. *Journal of Cross-Cultural Psychology, 15,* 111-138.

Singer, M. R. (1998). *Perception & identity in intercultural communication*. Yarmouth, ME: Intercultural Press.

Triandis, H. C., Vassiliou, V., Vassiliou, G., Tanaka, Y., & Shanmugam, A. V. (1972). *The analysis of subjective culture*. New York: Wiley.

Name _____   Date _____

Activity 1.3
UNDERSTANDING CULTURE THROUGH IDENTITY GROUPS

This activity is designed to encourage you to examine your cultural background by exploring your multiple group memberships. Marshall Singer (1998) has used the term *identity group* to refer to groups of people who perceive some aspect of the world similarly and who recognize and communicate about that similarity. According to Singer, the perceptions, values, attitudes, and beliefs that we learn from being a part of these groups, and the relative importance of our identity groups makes each of us culturally unique.

Directions: Think for a minute about your identity groups; that is, the group memberships that most clearly define who you are. These may include gender, nationality, religion, socioeconomic status, race, and ethnicity as well as such affiliations as political party, academic discipline, age cohort, disability status, sexual orientation, occupation, hobbies, and sports groups. Then answer the questions below in the space provided.

1. List your identity groups below:

_____   _____

_____   _____

_____   _____

_____   _____

_____   _____

2. Go back to your list of identity groups above and rank them by putting a (1) next to the group that you identify with most strongly, a (2) next to the group that is next most important to you, and so on.

3. Did you find the groups difficult to rank? Why or why not?

4. One reason that identity groups may be difficult to rank is that their importance may vary with the situation. Describe below a situation in which an identity group that you ranked as relatively unimportant might be more important to you.

5. Using the concept of identity groups, explain how we might improve our ability to communicate with culturally different others.

6. Using the concept of identity groups, describe the process of stereotyping and make a recommendation for decreasing one's tendency to stereotype culturally different others.

Reference:
    Singer, M. R. (1998). *Perception & identity in intercultural communication.* Yarmouth, ME: Intercultural Press.

Name _____   Date _____

Activity 1.4
A SEARCH FOR INDIVIDUALISM AND COLLECTIVISM

The concepts of individualism and collectivism have received great attention in recent research on culture and psychology. These terms stem from Geert Hofstede's (1980) classic cross-cultural study of workplace values. This activity encourages you to explore these concepts by seeking out written definitions and real-life examples of individualism and collectivism.

Directions: First use your textbook or library resources to locate definitions of individualism and collectivism (see Kim and colleagues [1994] and Triandis [1995] for more in-depth discussions of individualism and collectivism). Then identify one real-life example of individualism and one of collectivism. The ease with which you can find these examples will depend on whether you live in an individualistic or collectivistic culture. However, you should be able to find some forms of collectivism within an individualistic culture and some forms of individualism within a collectivist culture. Examples of individualism might include an advertisement for an electric blanket that has separate settings for the right and left sides of the blanket or a brochure for a preschool curriculum in which activities depend on the individual child's skills and interests. Examples of collectivism might include a beverage can designed to hold enough drink for two people to share or a T-shirt imprinted with the insignia of one's business. If possible, bring your examples in to class with this completed assignment.

1. Define *individualism* and provide a complete citation for the source of your definition.

2. Define *collectivism* and provide a complete citation for the source of your definition.

3. Describe your example of individualism and explain why it illustrates individualism.

4. Describe your example of collectivism and explain why it illustrates collectivism.

References:
    Hofstede, G. (1980). *Culture's consequences: International differences in work-related values.* Beverly Hills, CA: Sage.
    Kim, U., Triandis, H. C., Kagitcibasi, C., Choi, S.-C., & Yoon, G. (Eds.). (1994). *Individualism and collectivism: Theory, method, and applications.* Thousand Oaks, CA: Sage.
    Triandis, H. C. (1995). *Individualism and collectivism.* Greeley, CO: Westview.

Name _____   Date _____

Activity 1.5
SHOPPING FOR CULTURAL VALUES

Sometimes it is easier to identify the cultural values of groups that are more foreign to us than to identify cultural values that permeate our day to day environment. This activity is designed to give you some perspective on the values of the dominant culture in your society through a trip to your neighborhood supermarket or grocery store.

Directions: Select a supermarket or grocery store that is part of the dominant culture. Plan to spend 30 minutes to an hour making your observations. Take careful notes about the shoppers, the products available for purchase, and the layout of the store so that you can answer the questions below.

Name of store _____

Type of store _____

Time of day   _____

1. What type of food or products were most plentiful in the store? What type of food or products were scarce?

2. What claims were used to promote food items? Did these claims emphasize taste, nutritional value, cost, ease of preparation?

3. What were the most expensive items in the store? When a wide range of prices exists for the same type of product, what distinguished the lower from the higher cost versions?

4. What type of behavior did you observe on the part of the shoppers? Under what circumstances did shoppers interact with each other?

5. How were meats and poultry labeled and displayed? What efforts were made to distance these products from their original animal forms?

6. What did you observe about the sizes in which different types of products were available? What did these sizes imply about the social settings in which the products will be used?

7. How were foods from various ethnic groups distributed throughout the store? Were some ethnic foods presented as normative whereas others were presented as unusual or exotic?

8. What other observations did you make that informed you about cultural values?

9. Based on your answers to the questions above, what cultural values were evident in the supermarket setting?

10. Shalom Schwartz and colleagues have conducted extensive cross-cultural research on values. These studies support the existence of 10 *value types* across cultures. Although cultures may differ in terms of the degree to which specific values are endorsed, there appears to be a consistent structure to these values. Descriptions of the 10 value types are listed below (Schwartz & Sagiv, 1995).

- *Power:* Social status and prestige, control and dominance over people or resources.
- *Achievement:* Personal success through demonstrating competence according to social standards.
- *Hedonism:* Pleasure and sensuous gratification for oneself.
- *Stimulation:* Excitement, novelty, and challenge in life.
- *Self-Direction:* Independent thought, and action choosing, creating, exploring.
- *Universalism:* Understanding, appreciation, tolerance, and protection for the welfare of all people and for nature.
- *Benevolence:* Preservation and enhancement of the welfare of people with whom one is in frequent personal contact.
- *Tradition:* Respect, commitment, and acceptance of the customs and ideas that traditional culture or religion provide the self.
- *Conformity:* Restraint of actions, inclinations, and impulses likely to upset or harm others and violate social expectations or norms.
- *Security:* Safety, harmony, and stability of society, of relationships, and of self.

Which of these value types were most evident in the products and behaviors you observed in the grocery store? Please provide examples of the values that were expressed.

Source:

Descriptions of value types adapted from Schwartz, S., & Sagiv, L. Identifying culture-specifics in the content and structure of values. *Journal of Cross-Cultural Psychology, 26*, 92-116. Copyright (c) 1995 by Sage Publications, Inc.. Adapted with permission.

Name _____ Date _____

Activity 1.6
CLEANLINESS BELIEFS

One of the complaints sojourners often have when they visit another culture is that cleanliness practices are not adequate. This activity will help you to explore your own cleanliness beliefs and put them in cross-cultural perspective.

Directions: For each of the items below, circle the number to indicate your cleanliness beliefs. Where space is provided, respond to the follow-up question.

1. People in my culture value cleanliness.

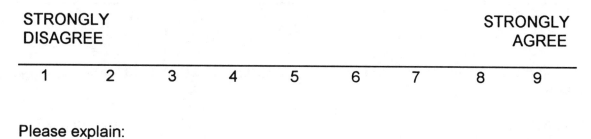

STRONGLY DISAGREE							STRONGLY AGREE	
1	2	3	4	5	6	7	8	9

Please explain:

2. One should wash one's body before entering a bathtub full of clean water.

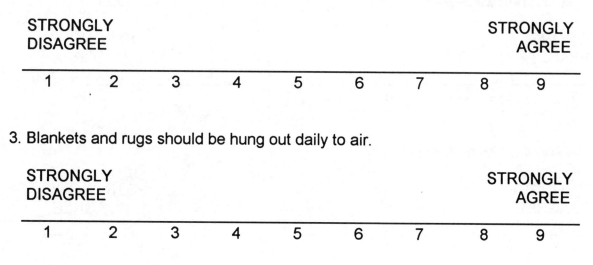

STRONGLY DISAGREE							STRONGLY AGREE	
1	2	3	4	5	6	7	8	9

3. Blankets and rugs should be hung out daily to air.

STRONGLY DISAGREE							STRONGLY AGREE	
1	2	3	4	5	6	7	8	9

4. Water should be used to clean oneself after using the toilet (rather than a "dry wipe").

STRONGLY   STRONGLY
DISAGREE   AGREE

| 1 | 2 | 3 | 4 | 5 | 6 | 7 | 8 | 9 |

5. Shoes should be removed before entering a home.

STRONGLY   STRONGLY
DISAGREE   AGREE

| 1 | 2 | 3 | 4 | 5 | 6 | 7 | 8 | 9 |

6. The left hand should not be used for eating or taking food from communal dishes.

STRONGLY   STRONGLY
DISAGREE   AGREE

| 1 | 2 | 3 | 4 | 5 | 6 | 7 | 8 | 9 |

7. One should use a different washcloth and bar of soap to wash oneself above the waist and below the waist.

STRONGLY   STRONGLY
DISAGREE   AGREE

| 1 | 2 | 3 | 4 | 5 | 6 | 7 | 8 | 9 |

8. One should shower or bathe daily.

STRONGLY   STRONGLY
DISAGREE   AGREE

| 1 | 2 | 3 | 4 | 5 | 6 | 7 | 8 | 9 |

9. Cleaning products should be used in the home to kill germs.

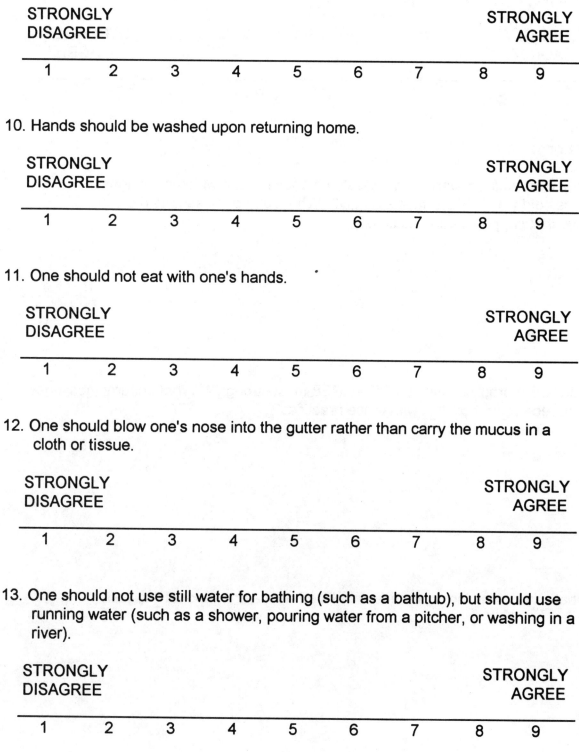

STRONGLY
DISAGREE

STRONGLY
AGREE

| 1 | 2 | 3 | 4 | 5 | 6 | 7 | 8 | 9 |

10. Hands should be washed upon returning home.

STRONGLY
DISAGREE

STRONGLY
AGREE

| 1 | 2 | 3 | 4 | 5 | 6 | 7 | 8 | 9 |

11. One should not eat with one's hands.

STRONGLY
DISAGREE

STRONGLY
AGREE

| 1 | 2 | 3 | 4 | 5 | 6 | 7 | 8 | 9 |

12. One should blow one's nose into the gutter rather than carry the mucus in a cloth or tissue.

STRONGLY
DISAGREE

STRONGLY
AGREE

| 1 | 2 | 3 | 4 | 5 | 6 | 7 | 8 | 9 |

13. One should not use still water for bathing (such as a bathtub), but should use running water (such as a shower, pouring water from a pitcher, or washing in a river).

STRONGLY
DISAGREE

STRONGLY
AGREE

| 1 | 2 | 3 | 4 | 5 | 6 | 7 | 8 | 9 |

14. The toilet should not be located under the same roof as the place where people eat and prepare food or sleep.

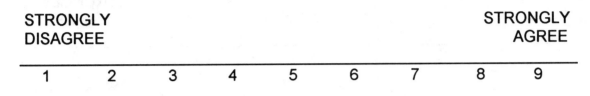

STRONGLY
DISAGREE

STRONGLY
AGREE

| 1 | 2 | 3 | 4 | 5 | 6 | 7 | 8 | 9 |

Reactions:

1. Look over your answers to the questions above. With which cleanliness practices did you AGREE most strongly? What cultural messages did you receive that support these practices?

2. With which practices did you DISAGREE most strongly? What cultural messages did you receive that conflict with these practices?

3. What other cleanliness practices not listed above are important to you?

4. How might someone from another culture feel about your beliefs if they endorse the practices with which you disagreed?

5. Look back at your response to item 1. Is there anything you would like to add to, or change in, your answer?

Sources:
    Based on Fernea, E., & Fernea, R. A. (1994). Cleanliness and culture. In W. J. Lonner & R. S. Malpass (Eds.), *Psychology and culture* (pp. 65-70). Boston: Allyn & Bacon, and
    Waxler-Morrison, N., Anderson, J., & Richardson, E. (1990). *Cross-cultural caring: A handbook for health professionals in Western Canada*. Vancouver, BC: University of British Columbia Press.

Name _____   Date _____

Activity 1.7
CULTURAL METAPHORS

Despite the large amount of information cross-cultural researchers have gathered, it is often difficult to convey to others exactly what a specific culture is like. Martin J. Gannon (1994) proposes the use of *cultural metaphors* as a way to easily express a cultural mindset and compare it to that of other cultures. These metaphors involve identifying an activity or phenomenon that most members of a culture would view as important, and then using it as a metaphor for describing key features of the cultural group. While cultural metaphors are generalizations and will not apply to all members of a group, these metaphors can provide a framework for beginning to understand and compare cultural groups. For example, Gannon uses the Turkish coffeehouse as a metaphor for understanding everyday life in Turkey. The coffeehouse metaphor has four main emphases:

- The formal and informal ties between Turkish coffeehouses and mosques, with which they typically share a portion of the town square, are similar to the nature of the coexistence of Islam and secular practices within Turkey.

- The Turkish coffeehouse functions as a place where group membership is valued and reinforced for the purposes of recreation, communication, and community integration, illustrating the Turkish group-oriented lifestyle.

- The Turkish coffeehouse is primarily a male domain symbolic of Turkey's male-dominated culture.

- The Turkish coffeehouse is characterized by simplicity, which reflects the Turkish emphasis on substance rather than form.

The purpose of this activity is to familiarize you with the concept of cultural metaphor and provide you with an experience constructing such metaphors.

Directions: Construct your own cultural metaphor for a culture with which you are familiar. You may select a culture based on nationality or may conceptualize culture more broadly to include other groups based on such dimensions as social class, age, gender, or ethnicity. You may even construct a metaphor to convey the essence of a student group such as a dormitory or sorority. Choose four or five dimensions of the culture to describe through your metaphor. Some suggestions for dimensions you might address are listed on page 24.

- basic values
- social structure
- view of cultural outsiders
- methods of socialization
- stressors and coping mechanisms

- gender roles
- work-related values
- communication style
- key events, holidays or activities
- rules for social interaction

In the space provided below, describe the culture you have selected and explain in some detail your cultural metaphor.

Source:
Based on Gannon, M. J. *Understanding global cultures: Metaphorical journeys through 17 countries.* Thousand Oaks, CA: Copyright (c) 1994 by Sage Publications, Inc. Adapted with permission.

Name _____ Date _____

Activity 1.8
CULTURAL RELATIVISM AND ETHNOCENTRISM

Most researchers of culture have adopted a philosophy of cultural relativism to some extent. *Cultural relativism* refers to the idea that behavior in a particular culture should not be judged by the standards of another culture. The extreme opposite of cultural relativism is ethnocentrism. An *ethnocentric* perspective uses the standards of one's own culture to judge the practices of a different culture. This activity encourages you to explore the complexities of the concepts of cultural relativism and ethnocentrism.

Directions: For each of the behaviors listed below, determine whether you would be likely to take the perspective of cultural relativism or ethnocentrism.

1. Although bullfighting is illegal in the United States, a bullfighting academy has been operating in Southern California. Though the students at this school do not train with real animals, the San Diego County Humane Society has threatened to cite the school for promoting animal cruelty. One of the founders of the academy takes the position that bullfighting is an important cultural practice and should not be prohibited.

Would you support cultural relativism or ethnocentrism in this case? Please explain.

2. Many cultures approve of polygynous marriages; that is, a man having more than one wife. Although it is considerably more rare, some cultures practice polyandry; that is, a woman having more than one husband.

Would you support cultural relativism or ethnocentrism in these cases? Please explain.

3. In some cultures eating dog meat is an acceptable practice. In fact, in response to a 1988 incident in which two Southeast Asian immigrants to the United States killed a German Shepard puppy for food, a state bill was passed prohibiting such behavior.

Would you support cultural relativism or ethnocentrism in this case? Please explain.

4. Millions of women and girls, primarily in the Middle East and Africa, have undergone the removal of parts of their genitalia as part of a traditional practice viewed by some as making them more respectable and marriageable. The procedure ranges from removal of the tip of the clitoris to infibulation in which the clitoris and labia are removed and the scraped sides of the vulva are joined together.

Would you support cultural relativism or ethnocentrism in this case? Please explain.

5. Some societies have rigid caste systems in which social hierarchy is maintained across generations. Caste membership is hereditary and generally involves restrictions on occupational choice and marriage partner.

Would you support cultural relativism or ethnocentrism in this case? Please explain.

6. There are currently over 450 hate groups operating in the United States. The cultural beliefs of these groups generally advocate white supremacy and are anti-Semitic and anti-gay.

Would you support cultural relativism or ethnocentrism in this case? Please explain.

Reactions: Based on your answers to the questions above, write a brief statement explaining the conditions under which you would take a culturally relativist or ethnocentric perspective when considering the practices of other cultures.

Name _____   Date _____

Activity 1.9
EXPLORING THE WORLD VILLAGE

This activity uses information from The World Village Project to help you view the population of the world from a more global perspective.

Directions: Imagine a village of 1,000 people that represents the planet Earth. Answer the questions below, assuming that all of the human ratios in the village were the same as those of the world.

Of the 1,000 inhabitants, indicate how many would fall into each of the following categories. Please see page 375 for the correct answers.

1. *Men and Women*
    _____ are men
    _____ are women

2. *Language*
    _____ speak Arabic   _____ speak Mandarin
    _____ speak English   _____ speak Russian
    _____ speak Hindi   _____ speak Spanish

3. *Religion*
    _____ are atheists   _____ are Jews
    _____ are Buddhists   _____ are Moslems
    _____ are Christians   _____ are non-religious
    _____ are Hindus   _____ are other religions

4. *Places of Origin*
    _____ are Africans   _____ are Latin Americans
    _____ are Asians   _____ are New Zealanders
    _____ are Australians   _____ are North Americans
    _____ are Europeans   _____ are Russians

5. *Age*

_____ are children

_____ are over the age of 65

6. *Daily Life*

_____ have access to clean drinking water

_____ live in substandard housing

_____ own automobiles

_____ own a computer

7. *Wealth*

_____ control 75% of the wealth

_____ receive 2% of the wealth

8. *Education*

_____ cannot read

_____ have a college education

Adapted from:
The World Village Project (www.worldvillage.org)

Name _____ Date _____

Activity 1.10
A GLOBAL VIEW OF PSYCHOLOGY

Most of what is published in psychology journals and textbooks takes a *Western* perspective (or *Western indigenous* perspective) and ignores the psychologies that have been developed by scholars across the globe to address concerns relevant to their own cultures. The purpose of this activity is twofold. First, it will acquaint you with some of the research interests of psychologists outside of Western Europe, the United States, and Canada. Second, it will encourage you to think about some of the influences on what is considered *Western psychology.**

Directions: For this activity you are asked to search a psychology database (such as PsycLIT or PsycINFO) to locate a journal article that focuses on research developed in a "non-Western" context. Such articles are often categorized under the heading of *indigenous psychology.*

1. Provide the complete citation for your article (see references at the end of activities in this book for examples of citation format and content).

2. In a paragraph or two, summarize this study. Include a description of the purpose of the study, participants, procedures, and results.

3. What social, cultural, political, historical, environmental, economic, or religious factors may have shaped the research focus of this study?

4. Look up the website of the American Psychological Association's International affairs office (at www.apa.org/ia). Describe below what you learned about the focus of psychology in a country other than your own.

5. What do you conclude about the social, cultural, political, historical, environmental, economic, or religious factors that may have shaped the research focus of Western psychology? Please explain.

* The term *Western psychology* can itself be viewed as ethnocentric in that it ignores the diverse cultures of the West and focuses only on those of European tradition.

Chapter 2. Culture and Psychological Research

Name _____   Date _____

Activity 2.1
FUNCTIONS OF CROSS-CULTURAL RESEARCH

As you have probably realized by now, cross-cultural research is not without its difficulties. Efforts must be made to identify appropriate cultures for testing a theory and to develop or select measures and procedures that will ensure cross-cultural comparisons are based on equivalent data. Why, then, would social scientists make the effort to conduct such research? Researchers choose to conduct cross-cultural studies for many different reasons. The purpose of this activity is to become familiar with the major functions of cross-cultural research.

Directions: Several functions of cross-cultural research have been identified and described (Lonner & Adamopoulos, 1997; Triandis, 1980). Read the functions of cross-cultural research listed below. Then, for each of the research project descriptions that follow, indicate which of the functions is served by taking a cross-cultural approach. More than one function may be relevant to some of the project descriptions.

Functions of Cross-Cultural Research

a. Identifying culture-specific values, cognitive categories, or forms of behavior.
b. Unconfounding variables. Two variables that may be linked in one culture may be unrelated in another culture.
c. Expanding the range of variables.
d. Understanding the relationship between ecological and psychological variables.
e. Identifying human universals.
f. Testing the generality of psychological models or theories.
g. Studying the effect of cultural change.

Project Descriptions:

1. A specialist in post-traumatic stress disorder constructed a model for predicting the likelihood that someone will develop psychological disturbances in response to extreme trauma. His original model was based on a study of survivors of war-related incidents in Northern Ireland. He wondered if his model would also be a good predictor in other cultures, so he tested it on a similar population in Mozambique.

What function was served by taking a cross-cultural approach? Please explain.

2. A community psychologist was interested in the effect of neighborhood stability on willingness to participate in community-based environmental programs. She was having some difficulty conducting her research because in her own culture most neighborhoods were relatively unstable. By including several other cultures in her study, she was able to explore "willingness to participate" within unstable, moderately stable, and highly stable neighborhoods.

What function was served by taking a cross-cultural approach? Please explain.

3. A social psychologist was studying the impact of exposure to television on children's beliefs about the value of material goods. In her own culture, only wealthy families own televisions, thus causing difficulty in separating the effects of television viewing from the effects of growing up in a wealthy family. Instead, she decided to conduct her research in the United States where she could find children with different levels of exposure to television at both high and low income levels.

What function was served by taking a cross-cultural approach? Please explain.

4. An experimental psychologist was interested in the effect of urban living on depth perception. He reasoned that city dwellers might be less sensitive than people in rural environments to depth cues that involve distance. He used stimuli to assess the perception of depth cues with individuals living in cultures based in a variety of urban and rural environments.

What function was served by taking a cross-cultural approach? Please explain.

5. An interdisciplinary team of researchers was exploring the reasons why members of certain ethnic groups were underrepresented as clients of a neighborhood mediation center. They hypothesized that the techniques used at the mediation center may be culturally inappropriate for some people. Instead of encouraging members of those groups to use the mediation center, they decided to conduct a cross-cultural study to try to identify methods of resolving disputes that were indigenous to those ethnic groups.

What function was served by taking a cross-cultural approach? Please explain.

6. A clinical psychologist was interested in the impact of racial oppression on self-concept. Because changes in racial oppression were more subtle in his own culture, he decided to conduct a study in South Africa in which he compared pre- and post-Apartheid indices of self-esteem among school children.

What function was served by taking a cross-cultural approach? Please explain.

7. A student of psychology examined crime statistics in her country and noticed that far more violent criminal acts were committed by males than by females. She wondered if this might be due to biological differences or whether it reflected gender differences in experience (such as childrearing, the media, toys, or peer influences). When she looked to the cross-cultural literature she found a large number of studies from different parts of the world reporting findings that males exhibited higher rates of aggression than females.

What function was served by taking a cross-cultural approach? Please explain.

References:
   Lonner, W. J., & Adamopoulos, J. (1997). Culture as antecedent to behavior. In J. W. Berry, Y. H. Poortinga, & J. Pandey (Eds.), *Handbook of cross-cultural psychology: Vol 1. Theory and method* (2nd ed., pp. 43-83). Boston: Allyn & Bacon.
   Triandis, H. C. (1980). Introduction to handbook of cross-cultural psychology. In H. C. Triandis & W. W. Lambert (Eds.), *Handbook of cross-cultural psychology: Vol. 1. Perspectives* (pp. 1-14). Boston: Allyn & Bacon.

Name _____   Date _____

Activity 2.2
INSIDERS AND OUTSIDERS

Psychologists have long emphasized objectivity in research and have expressed concern about bias that stems from the researcher being too close to the groups they are studying. In contrast, anthropologists have traditionally taken an approach that involves taking part in the circumstances one is describing or analyzing. What are the advantages of being a cultural outsider or a cultural insider? This activity is designed to clarify differences between the insider perspective and the outsider perspective in conducting cross-cultural research.

Directions: Find an organized group or club that is well known on or off your campus. Identify two people to interview about this group: one who is a member (an insider) and one who is not (an outsider). Ask the same questions outlined below to both interviewees. Please assure your respondents that their identities will remain confidential. Do not include their names on these sheets.

Group: _____

Interview A: Insider (Member)

1. How did you first learn about this group?

2. What are the criteria for membership?

3. How would you characterize the members of this group?

4. What are the goals of this group?

5. How effective is this group in achieving their goals? Please explain.

6. What is the perception most nonmembers have of this group?

Interview B: Outsider (Nonmember)

1. How did you first learn about this group?

2. What are the criteria for membership?

3. How would you characterize the members of this group?

4. What are the goals of this group?

5. How effective is this group in achieving their goals? Please explain.

6. What is the perception most nonmembers have of this group?

Reactions: First compare the responses from the two interviews, then answer the questions below.

1. Describe the major differences between the two accounts.

2. What are the advantages and disadvantages of using insiders as an information source?

3. What are the advantages and disadvantages of using outsiders as an information source?

4. What would you recommend for cross-cultural psychologists in terms of being an insider or outsider relative to the cultures they study?

Name _____   Date _____

Activity 2.3
EMIC AND ETIC PERSPECTIVES

The purpose of this activity is to familiarize you with a key concept in studying culture and human behavior; the distinction between *emics* and *etics*. According to Berry (1969), etic research focuses on human universals, whereas emic research addresses the way these universal behaviors are expressed in specific cultures. Berry warns us about the danger of an *imposed etic* in which we assume that research concepts or methodologies developed in North American universities have the same meaning in other cultural groups. For example, people in all cultures make moral judgments, but a cross-cultural study that measures Kohlberg's stages of moral development across cultures is using an imposed etic. Instead, it may be possible to identify emic forms of moral behavior, such as *ahimsa*, an Indian principle of nonviolence based on respect for all life (Eckensberger & Zimba, 1997).

Directions: First add five etics to the list below. Then choose one of these etics, select a cultural group with which you are familiar, and describe the associated emic for that cultural group.

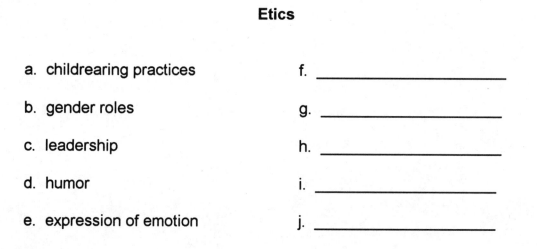

Etics

a. childrearing practices   f. _____

b. gender roles   g. _____

c. leadership   h. _____

d. humor   i. _____

e. expression of emotion   j. _____

1. Identify the etic you selected.

2. Describe an associated emic.

Reference:
    Berry, J. W. (1969). On cross-cultural comparability. *International Journal of Psychology, 4*, 119-128.
    Eckensberger, L. H., & Zimba, R. F. (1997). The development of moral judgment. In J. W. Berry, P. R. Dasen, & T. S. Saraswathi (Eds.), *Handbook of cross-cultural psychology: Vol. 2. Basic processes and human development* (2nd ed., pp.299-338). Boston: Allyn & Bacon.

Name _____   Date _____

Activity 2.4
MEASURING ETHNIC IDENTITY

Researchers of culture and psychology often include in their studies a measure of ethnic identity. Sometimes ethnic identity takes the form of an independent variable. In other words, some phenomenon (for example, conflict resolution style) is predicted to vary by ethnicity. Sometimes ethnic identity is a dependent variable. That is, some other variable is predicted to have an effect on ethnic identity. For example, one might hypothesize that urban dwelling and rural dwelling Canadian Indians might differ in ethnic identity. This activity encourages you to explore some of the ways ethnic identity is measured and to think critically about the validity of these measurement techniques.

Directions: In response to the items below, develop different measurements of ethnic identity. You need not actually administer these measures, but might think about how people with various ethnic backgrounds might respond to your measures.

Measurements:
1. Write a free-response questionnaire item (an item that does not give any options, but is open ended) asking the respondent to simply state his or her ethnic identity.

2. Write a questionnaire item that asks the respondent to report his or her ethnic ancestry in terms of a proportional representation of his or her parents' or grandparents' ethnicity (in terms of fractions or percentages).

3. Write a questionnaire item that includes a checklist of ethnic categories from which the respondent chooses in order to indicate his or her ethnic identity.

4. For this question only, you are asked to think about how you would measure the degree to which someone identifies with a *specific* ethnic group. Write a questionnaire item that asks the respondent about behaviors (such as food, hobbies, reading material, or cultural practices) that are seen as indicative of a particular ethnic identity. For example, a behavioral measure of French Canadian ethnic identity might be "Do you subscribe to a French language newspaper?" Specify below the ethnic identity you are assessing and write at least five behavioral items for that cultural group.

Application:

1. Give an example of a research problem that could be tested using the free-response measure.

2. Give an example of a research problem that could be tested using the proportional ancestry measure.

3. Give an example of a research problem that could be tested using the checklist measure.

4. Give an example of a research problem that could be tested using the behavioral measure.

Reactions:

1. Which of the four measures do you view as generally the most accurate way to assess ethnic identity? The least accurate? Please explain.

2. Which type of measure best assesses *your* ethnic identity. Please explain.

Name _____ Date _____

Activity 2.5
WRITING TRANSLATABLE ITEMS

There is much controversy among those who study culture and psychology over the wisdom of using materials developed in one culture to assess the behaviors of individuals in another culture. However, most would agree that if translation is to be used, there are practices that increase its accuracy. The purpose of this activity is to explore the process of preparing test materials for translation.

Directions: Using library resources (such as PsycLIT or PsycINFO), locate a scale or test that is designed to measure some psychological phenomenon. Two good sources to help you identify tests in your area of interest are the *Mental Measurements Yearbook*, which contains descriptions, reviews, and references for hundreds of tests, and *Tests in Print*, which is a bibliography of commercially available tests. Once you have located a scale, choose five items of interest to you and write them below. Next, modify the wording of the items based on the rules on page 50 extracted from Brislin, Lonner, and Thorndike's (1973) guidelines for writing translatable items.

1. State the author, source, and name of the scale.

2. List five of the original scale items.

   a.

   b.

   c.

   d.

   e.

Guidelines for writing translatable items:
1. Use short, simple sentences.
2. Use active rather than passive words.
3. Repeat nouns instead of using pronouns.
4. Avoid metaphor and colloquialisms.
5. Avoid the subjunctive tense (such as verb forms with *could* or *would*).
6. Avoid adverbs and prepositions telling where or when (such as *frequent, beyond, upper*).
7. Avoid possessive forms.
8. Use specific rather than general terms (such as *cow, chicken,* or *pig* rather than *livestock*).
9. Avoid words indicating vagueness regarding some event or thing (such as *probably* or *frequently*)
10. Avoid sentences with two different verbs if the verbs indicate two different actions.

3. List the five modified items.

a.

b.

c.

d.

e.

Source:
    Guidelines for writing translatable items adapted from Brislin, R., Lonner, W., & Thorndike, R. *Cross-cultural research methods.* Copyright (c) 1973 by John Wiley & Sons, Inc. Adapted with permission.

Name _____   Date _____

Activity 2.6
BACK TRANSLATION

One of the many concerns in conducting cross-cultural research is the accuracy of translated materials. This activity will provide you with an opportunity to try out a widely used technique for improving the quality of translated materials called *back translation* (Brislin, 1980).

Directions: For this activity you will need to enlist the help of two bilingual individuals who are skilled in the same languages. The materials to be translated are the five test items you developed in Activity 2.5 or any other five psychological test items. The first bilingual individual is to translate the test items from the original language to a second (or target) language. You are then to hand the translated version to a second bilingual individual who is to translate them back into their original language. The two bilingual assistants are to work separately on this task. By comparing the original and back-translated version of the test items you can identify concepts or word forms that cannot be accurately translated.

1. State the author, source, and name of the scale.

2. What is the target language for your translation?

3. List your five items from Activity 2.5 or other source.

    a.

    b.

    c.

    d.

    e.

4. List the items as translated into the target language.

    a.

    b.

    c.

    d.

    e.

5. List the five items as back translated into the original language.

    a.

    b.

    c.

    d.

    e.

6. List below any words or phrases that did not translate accurately. What insights about cultural differences do these problems in translation provide?

7. Based on the results of the back translation, are their any modifications you think would be useful to make to the *original* version to allow for a translation into comparable versions? Please explain.

8. Assuming an accurate translation is achieved, what other concerns might you have about using the original and translated versions of this scale to conduct cross-cultural research?

Reference:

Brislin, R. (1980). Translation and content analysis of oral and written materials. In H. Triandis and J. Berry (Eds.), *Handbook of cross-cultural psychology: Vol.2: Methodology* (pp.389-444). Boston: Allyn & Bacon.

Name _____ Date _____

Activity 2.7
PAGTATANONG-TANONG:
AN INDIGENOUS RESEARCH METHOD

This activity evaluates the cross-cultural applicability of the research methods typically used in "Western psychology" and explores an indigenous research method from the Philippines called *Pagtatanong-tanong*.

Directions: Read the scenario and answer the questions that follow.

Scenario: Suppose that you have been trained at your university to uphold the following principles of research:

- The researcher must remain objective. It is important not to become too emotionally attached, or disclose personal information, to research participants.

- Procedures should be standardized. The questions asked of participants and the conditions under which they are asked should be as uniform as possible.

- Participants should not be subject to the influence of others during the testing or interview process (unless it is a condition of the experiment). Thus, participants should be tested or interviewed on an individual basis.

Imagine that you are preparing to conduct a series of interviews in a rural community in the Philippines. Through reading and speaking with experts and members of this community you learn the following about the culture in which you are planning to conduct your research.

- People are unaccustomed to being asked a series of questions in sequence and responding in a regimented manner.

- People are uncomfortable discussing personal opinions or behaviors with a stranger with whom there will be no future relationship.

- People are more comfortable speaking in a conversational manner in which each person discloses information and manages the process and content of the conversation.

- People may be uncomfortable alone with a stranger, particularly if the stranger is of a different gender or social status.

1. Describe how you might modify your research methods in order to effectively conduct your interviews. Which research principles would you be willing to reconsider and which principles would you continue to uphold?

Pe-Pua (1989) and others have described a social science research method indigenous to the Philippines called *Pagtatanong-tanong*. According to Pe-Pua, Pagtatanong-tanong has some of the following characteristics:

- The researcher uses a tentative outline of questions that are revised based on input from the participants.

- The researcher and the participants share equally in determining the content and structure of the interview.

- A relationship is established between the researcher and the participants such that the participants feel comfortable asking the researcher questions and expect that they may have contact with the researcher in the future.

- The researcher starts interviewing with a group of participants. Interruptions in the interview process are not seen as distractions, but as an opportunity to check on the reliability of information obtained.

2. What do you expect about the validity of the information you would collect in the rural community in the Philippines using the Pagtatanong-tanong method?

3. If you are not from the rural Philippines, do you think that Pagtatanong-tanong would yield useful information in your culture? Please explain.

Reference:
   Pe-Pua, R. (1989). Pagtatanong-tanong: A cross-cultural research method. *International Journal of Intercultural Relations, 13*, 147-163.

Name _____   Date _____

Activity 2.8
ETHICS IN CROSS-CULTURAL RESEARCH

You are probably familiar with many of the ethical concerns faced by psychologists, such as obtaining informed consent from potential research participants, protecting them from harm and discomfort, and fully debriefing participants once the research has been completed. This activity encourages you to think about the additional ethical issues cross-cultural psychologists must address.

Directions: Read the following scenario and identify any ethical dilemmas. Next, propose an alternative research design that will remedy each ethical concern.

Scenario: A study conducted in the United States by Carolyn Keating and Karen Heltman (1994) indicated that children and men who convincingly deceive others also tend to be leaders in a group context. These findings did not hold true for women. Suppose an American social psychologist is interested in the cross-cultural applicability of these findings. He wonders if the gender differences identified in this study would also occur in a more collectivist setting. He reasons that the group dynamics experienced by both males and females in a collectivist culture may be more similar to the group dynamics experienced by women in Keating's study. The researcher obtains a government grant to conduct his study in a small, collectivist Pacific Island community. His study identifies individuals who are able to deceive others effectively and explores the degree to which these individuals hold leadership roles. He documents his findings with both written and video records. Early in the research process he befriends a local high school teacher and soon involves him in the research. Though an official of the local government has volunteered his assistance, the researcher finds the teacher easier to talk to and declines the government official's offer. The teacher takes primary responsibility for identifying potential research participants, translating data, and acting as a liaison with local authorities. The teacher also spends a considerable amount of time discussing possible interpretations of the data with the researcher. Both the teacher and the research participants are compensated at the rate of $7.00 per hour, a large amount in terms of the local economy, since this is the same amount the researcher has paid participants in the United States. Once the study is completed, the researcher presents his findings to the community then returns to the United States to present his findings at a national conference, using the video materials as illustration. A few months later, he is sole author of a journal article reporting the results of this study.

1. Discuss each of the ethical concerns illustrated by the above scenario.

2. Propose an alternative research design to remedy the ethical limitations of this study.

Reference:
   Keating, C. F., & Heltman, K. R. (1994). Dominance and deception in children and adults: Are leaders the best misleaders? *Personality and Social Psychology Bulletin, 20,* 312-321.

Name _____   Date _____

Activity 2.9
TOWARD A MORE INCLUSIVE PSYCHOLOGY

If psychology as a discipline is to become more inclusive and less culturally biased, those who read and conduct psychological research will need to become better able to identify and avoid bias in the design of psychological research. The purpose of this activity is to familiarize you with some of the forms of bias that frequently occur in studying psychological processes.

Directions: Read the research project descriptions below and identify the form(s) of bias in each.

1. In a study of attachment behavior and academic self-concept, children and their mothers are observed and interviewed at great length to determine the nature and degree of the bond between them.

2. A researcher is interested in exploring an association between sexual orientation and strategies for coping with stress. She sends a brief questionnaire to two groups of women. One group was selected from the members of the Gay and Lesbian Alumni Association of her university, the other from individuals who had indicated on a recent alumni survey that they are married.

3. A researcher is interested in studying social interaction between people with and without disabilities. He simulates disability by having a nondisabled student confederate sit in a wheelchair in the snack bar of the student center and then observes the interaction between the confederate and the (nondisabled) students who enter the room.

4. A journal specializing in gender issues in psychology devotes an entire issue to the topic of Asian and Pacific women.

5. A study of friendship patterns in adults compares results across four different age groups. The groups consist of 18 to 29 year-olds, 30 to 45 year-olds, 46 to 59 year-olds, and individuals over 60.

Sources:
   Project descriptions based, respectively, on the following articles:
   Denmark, F. L. (1994). Engendering psychology. *American Psychologist, 49*, 329-334.
   Fine, M., & Asch, A. (1988). Disability beyond stigma: Social interaction, discrimination, and activism. *Journal of Social Issues, 44*, 3-21.
   Herek, G., Kimmel, D. L., Amaro, H., & Melton, G. B. (1991). Avoiding heterosexist bias in psychological research. *American Psychologist, 46*, 957-963.
   Reid, P. T., & Kelly, K. (1994). Research on women of color: From ignorance to awareness. *Psychology of Women Quarterly, 18*, 477-486.
   Schaie, K. W. (1988). Ageism in psychological research. *American Psychologist, 43*, 179-183.

Name _____   Date _____

Activity 2.10
DESIGNING CROSS-CULTURAL RESEARCH

Designing research that compares cultures on some psychological phenomenon involves several steps beyond what is required for research within a single culture. It rarely makes sense to conduct the study in exactly the same way using exactly the same materials in more that one culture. Although the studies in each culture cannot be the *same*, it is important that they be *equivalent.* This activity will acquaint you with some of the forms of equivalence that must be considered in conducting cross-cultural research.

Directions: For this activity you will need to locate a journal article that reports a psychological study conducted within a single culture. Try to choose a relatively straightforward study in which the independent and dependent variables, the hypothesis, and the methods used are understandable to you. Determine in which culture you would replicate the study. In practice, the choice of cultures in which to conduct research should be based on aspects of the cultures that are relevant to the theories or concepts you are testing. For this activity, however, it is more important that you choose a culture that is somewhat familiar to you. Next, answer the questions below regarding various issues of cross-cultural equivalence.

1. Provide the complete citation for the journal article you have chosen.

2. Briefly describe the study that you will prepare to replicate. Include the independent and dependent variables, the hypothesis, and the methods used.

3. Describe the culture in which the above study would be replicated.

Equivalence: For each of the following forms of equivalence, determine whether the procedures used in the original study would be culturally appropriate if used in the second culture. If the procedure is not appropriate, suggest how you might modify the procedure in order to produce an outcome that is equivalent in both cultures.

1. *Conceptual Equivalence.* Do the primary phenomena being investigated have the same meaning in both cultures? For example, the concept of *parenting behavior* may not have conceptual equivalence if comparing a culture in which parents are the primary caregivers and a culture in which the extended family or siblings play a major role in childrearing.

2. *Sampling Equivalence.* Does the method of recruiting research participants yield individuals who are similar on dimensions other than culture? For example, many studies are conducted with college students as participants. However, college students in a culture where a large proportion of the population attends college may differ in important ways from students in a culture where only the most privileged attend college.

3. *Item or Task Equivalence*. Do the questionnaire or interview items or experimental tasks that participants perform have the same meaning in both cultures? For example, an altruism questionnaire that asks whether one is willing to call the police may not have similar meaning for groups of high and low socioeconomic status due to differences in past experiences with police.

4. *Equivalence of the Test Situation*. Is the test situation likely to be perceived and valued similarly in both cultures? For example, in some cultures people are very familiar with strangers approaching them to ask somewhat personal questions as part of a study. In other cultures this is a circumstance that would elicit suspicion and concern.

Chapter 3. Culture and Basic Processes

Name _____   Date _____

Activity 3.1
MAGICAL THINKING

Sometimes members of more traditional cultures are described as using forms of magical thinking that defy rules of logic and reason. Paul Rozin, Linda Millman, and Carol Nemeroff (1986) suggest that such thinking is not limited to traditional cultures, but exists in some aspects of daily life in highly industrialized cultures as well. Their research on college students in the United States indicates the two forms of magical thinking below, described a century ago by Sir James Frazer (1890/1959).

The law of contagion states that when two things (or beings) are in contact with each other the properties of one can permanently transfer to the other. For example, Frazer describes an ancient Chinese practice in which burial clothes were sewn by young women with the reasoning that their longevity would somehow pass into the clothes and ensure that the clothes themselves would live long (that is, not be used for many years).

The law of similarity holds that an image of an object or person takes on the characteristics of the actual object or person. For example, Frazer notes that in many cultures it was believed that by injuring footprints it is possible to injure the feet that made them.

The purpose of this activity is to explore the use of magical thinking among college students and consider the meaning of such thinking for understanding the link between culture and cognition.

Directions: Identify two college students to act as participants in this activity. Then, using the interview forms below, ask each participant the two questions about magical thinking based on the study by Rozin and colleagues. Please interview the two participants separately and do not tell them that you are studying magical thinking. The first item addresses the law of contagion and the second item addresses the law of similarity.

Participant A

1. Would you rather wear a laundered shirt that had been previously worn by someone you like, someone you dislike, or someone you don't know? Please explain.

2. Would it be more difficult for you to throw darts at a dartboard depicting a picture of someone you like or someone you don't like? Please explain.

Participant B

1. Would you rather wear a laundered shirt that had been previously worn by someone you like, someone you dislike, or someone you don't know? Please explain.

2. Would it be more difficult for you to throw darts at a dartboard depicting a picture of someone you like or someone you don't like? Please explain.

Reactions:

1. To what extent did your participants manifest magical thinking (on item 1, choosing the shirt worn by the liked person, and on item 2, having more difficulty throwing darts at the liked person, indicates magical thinking).

2. Can you think of any alternative explanations for the "magical thinking" in the two questions asked of the participants?

3. Have you engaged in any other forms of magical thinking? Please explain.

4. To what extent does magical thinking interfere with rational thinking in everyday life in your culture?

Source:
Based on Rozin, P., Millman, L., & Nemeroff, C. (1986). Operation of the laws of sympathetic magic in disgust and other domains. *Journal of Personality and Social Psychology, 50*, 703-712.

References:
Frazer, J. G. (1959). *The new golden bough: A study in magic and religion.* New York: MacMillan (Edited by T. H. Gaster, 1922; Original work published 1890).
Rozin, P., Millman, L., & Nemeroff, C. (1986). Operation of the laws of sympathetic magic in disgust and other domains. *Journal of Personality and Social Psychology, 50*, 703-712.

Name _____   Date _____

Activity 3.2
IMPLICIT THEORIES OF INTELLIGENCE

Patricia Ruzgis and Elena Grigorenko (1994) distinguish between cross-cultural research that focuses on explicit and implicit theories of intelligence. They explain that studies of explicit theories have attempted to determine how cultural environments impact the development of different patterns of intellectual abilities. The data used to test explicit theories usually consists of scores on various tests of cognitive abilities. Explicit theories are constructed by specialists in investigating cognitive abilities. Implicit theories, on the other hand, are the ideas that everyday people have about what constitutes intelligence. Data gathered to study implicit theories may consist of characteristics of an intelligent person or definitions of intelligence generated by research participants. Ruzgis and Grigorenko note Irvine's (1970) emphasis on the importance of studying implicit theories of intelligence in order to understand cultural differences in conceptions of intelligence. In this activity, you can explore your own implicit theory of intelligence and compare it to data on implicit theories of intelligence across cultures. We will also examine the concept of *giftedness* as a way to gain further insight into conceptions of intelligence.

Directions: Please respond to each of the questions below in the space provided.

1. Describe what the term *intelligent* means to you.

2. Describe what the term *gifted* means to you.

3. Read the list of behaviors, skills, and abilities below. Put an 'X' in the blank next to any item you associate with *an intelligent person*.

_____ a. reasons logically
_____ b. is verbally fluent
_____ c. is sociable
_____ d. can take another's point of view
_____ e. works efficiently
_____ f. identifies connections among ideas
_____ g. speaks clearly and articulately
_____ h. is humorous
_____ i. is modest
_____ j. plans ahead
_____ k. sees all aspects of a problem
_____ l. is knowledgeable about a particular field of study
_____ m.gets along well with others
_____ n. admits mistakes in good grace
_____ o. makes clear decisions

4. For each of the items you selected above, add a point to the appropriate subscale below and calculate your scores for each of the five subscales (your scores should range from 0 to 3).

_____ Practical Problem Solving: items a., f., and k.

_____ Verbal Ability: items b., g., and l.

_____ Positive Social Competence: items c., h., and m.

_____ Receptive Social Competence: items d., i., and n.

_____ Task Efficiency: items e., j., and o.

5. Azuma and Kashiwagi (1987) distinguished between positive social competence and receptive social competence.   Look at the items that compose each of these subscales. How would you describe the difference between these two forms of social competence?

6. Look at your scores on the Positive Social Competence and Receptive Social Competence subscales. To what extent were these subscales part of your image of an intelligent person?

7. Ruzgis and Grigorenko have observed that positive social competence corresponds to the social component in implicit theories of intelligence studied in such individualistic cultures as Australia, Canada, and the United States. These authors note that receptive social competence tends to correspond to the social component in implicit theories of intelligence in the collectivist cultures such as among Asian and African societies. Why might Positive Social Competence be associated with individualism and Receptive Social Competence be associated with collectivism?

8. Sternberg, Conway, Ketron, and Bernstein (1981) explored the implicit theories of intelligence held by American laypersons and experts (researchers of human intelligence). They found that the laypersons' conceptions could be categorized into three categories: Practical Problem Solving, Verbal Ability, and Social Competence (this latter category is not included in the subscales above, but was more similar to Positive Social Competence than Receptive Social Competence). For the experts, however, social competence was not included in conceptions of intelligence! How might you explain this distinction between the laypersons' and experts' views of intelligence?

9. Reread your description of intelligence in question 1. Are there any characteristics in your description that would not be categorized under any of the five subscales? Please explain.

10. Cross-cultural researchers have observed much variability in cultural conceptions of giftedness including some cultures in which there is no term for giftedness. For example, Mary Romero (1994) explored the underrepresentation of American Indian children in gifted and talented programs, specifically in regard to Keresan Pueblo society. She found that the Keresan concept of giftedness reflected the collectivism of Keresan society. Giftedness required that one's unique talents or abilities contributed to the well-being of the community. Furthermore, giftedness in Keresan society did not involve distinguishing one individual over another. Reread your description of giftedness in question 2. To what extent does your description reflect individualist values? Collectivist values?

11. Discuss the implications of cultural differences in the meaning of intelligence for cross-cultural research on *explicit* theories of intelligence.

Source:

The Positive Social Competence, Receptive Social Competence, and Task Efficiency items were derived from Azuma, H. & Kashiwagi, K. Descriptors for an intelligent person: A Japanese Study. *Japanese Psychological Research, 29,* 17-26. Copyright (c) 1987 by Japanese Psychological Association. Adapted with permission.

The Practical Problem Solving and Verbal Ability items were derived from Sternberg, R. J., Conway, B. E., Ketron, J. L., & Bernstein, M. People's conceptions of intelligence. *Journal of Personality and Social Psychology, 41,* 37-55. Copyright (c) 1981 by American Psychological Association. Adapted with permission.

References:

Azuma, H., & Kashiwagi, K., (1987). Descriptors for an intelligent person: A Japanese Study. *Japanese Psychological Research, 29,* 17-26.

Irvine, S. H. (1970). Affect and construct -- a cross-cultural check on theories of intelligence. *Journal of Social Psychology, 80,* 23-30.

Romero, M. E., (1994). Identifying giftedness among Keresan Pueblo Indians: The Keres Study. *Journal of American Indian Education, 34,* 35-58.

Ruzgis, P., & Grigorenko, E. L. (1994). Cultural meaning systems, intelligence, and personality. In R. J. Sternberg & P. Ruzgis (Eds.), *Personality and intelligence* (pp. 248-270). New York: Cambridge University Press.

Sternberg, R. J., Conway, B. E., Ketron, J. L., & Bernstein, M. (1981). People's conceptions of intelligence. *Journal of Personality and Social Psychology, 41,* 37-55.

Name _____   Date _____

Activity 3.3
CULTURE AND INTELLIGENCE:
EVALUATING *THE BELL CURVE*

In 1994, Richard J, Herrnstein and Charles Murray published a controversial book entitled, *The Bell Curve: Intelligence and Class Structure in American Life.* In this book, these authors argue the following:

- There are racial differences in IQ, with Asians scoring about three points higher than white Americans, who in turn average 15 points higher than Black Americans.

- Racial differences in IQ are largely determined by genetics.

- IQ is a better predictor than socioeconomic status of social behaviors (such as crime, unemployment, and births out of wedlock).

- IQ predicts socioeconomic success and will become a more critical predictor of success in the future as high status positions become more complex and require more credentials.

- IQ is immutable (cannot be changed), therefore educational intervention programs designed to improve cognitive abilities should be eliminated.

- Black people will be increasingly limited to low income/low status positions in the future.

Many scholars have criticized the logic and use of scientific method that forms the foundation of *The Bell Curve*. In fact, John Carey (1995, pp. 54-55) writes that ". . . there's a grim sport for sharp-eyed readers in spotting the weak links, misrepresentations, and logical inconsistencies that riddle the supposedly objective analysis of the data." This activity requires that you critically evaluate the assumptions underlying the logic of *The Bell Curve*.

Directions: Write a brief (one page) essay supporting or refuting one of the assumptions below. Locate and cite at least two scholarly sources (books or journal articles) to back your position.

- High IQ leads to (causes) socioeconomic success.

- It is scientifically valid to examine "racial differences."

- IQ test scores indicate fundamental intellectual ability.

- Racial differences in IQ reflect genetic differences.

- IQ is immutable.

Essay:

References:
   Carey, J. (1995). Clever arguments, atrocious science. In R. Jacoby & N. Glauberman (Eds.), *The bell curve debate* (pp. 53-56). New York: Random House. (Originally published 1994).
   Herrnstein, R. J., & Murray, C. (1994). *The bell curve: Intelligence and class structure in American life.* New York: The Free Press.

Name _____   Date _____

Activity 3.4
TESTING COGNITIVE ABILITIES ACROSS CULTURES

One difference of opinion between cultural psychologists and cross-cultural psychologists has to do with perceptions of the usefulness of testing cognitive abilities (such as problem solving, memory, and categorization) across cultures (Greenfield, 1997). *Cross-cultural psychologists* have tended to believe that once adjustments are made to a cognitive abilities test it can be effectively used in a culture other than the one for which it was originally developed. In fact, a significant portion of cross-cultural psychology focuses on how to modify tests (such as through translation or the use of culturally familiar materials and tasks) in order to make them cross-culturally appropriate. *Cultural psychologists*, on the other hand, tend to believe that cognitive ability tests are themselves a product of culture. Patricia Greenfield (1997) explains that *symbolic culture*-- that is, shared assumptions, knowledge, and communication-- is imbedded in any test of cognitive ability. She argues that if the individuals tested do not share the symbolic culture of the test or tester, the result will be cultural misunderstandings that threaten the validity of the test. Greenfield recommends an alternative to taking tests from one culture and using it in another. She suggests that one should first identify cognitive abilities that are valued within a particular culture and then develop culturally appropriate ways to measure these indigenous cognitive skills. This strategy might be called an *emic*, or culture-specific, approach. The purpose of this activity is to examine how one might go about using the cultural psychologists' approach to studying cognitive abilities.

Directions: Imagine that you have been hired to develop a test of cognitive ability to be used in a culture where formal testing has never taken place.

1. Describe how you would go about determining which abilities are valued in this culture.

2. Describe how you would develop a measure to test those abilities.

3. Under what circumstances might it be appropriate to use a standardized cognitive abilities test (such as an IQ test) in the culture described above?

Reference:
    Greenfield, P. M. (1997). You can't take it with you: Why ability assessments don't cross cultures. *American Psychologist, 52,* 1115-1124.

Name _____   Date _____

Activity 3.5
VIDEO GAMES AS CULTURAL ARTIFACTS

Researchers have frequently confronted findings that indicate large discrepancies between the abilities people demonstrate in laboratory studies and those the same people demonstrate in real life. For example, Nunes (1995) found that child vendors in Brazilian markets demonstrated mathematical abilities that were not expressed in test situations. Such findings have prompted social scientists to explore the skills people learn and demonstrate in the context of daily life, termed *everyday cognition* (Schliemann, Carraher, & Ceci, 1997). Patricia Greenfield (1994) has described a form of everyday cognition that involves interacting with a specific type of cultural artifact-- the action video game. Greenfield has outlined a series of competencies required for, and developed from, experience with video games. The purpose of this activity is to explore video games as a form of everyday cognition that prepares children for effective functioning as adults in your culture.

Directions: Play and observe others playing an action video game either on a home computer or game system or in a public setting. Then describe the game below and answer the questions that follow.

Video Game Description (include the name of the game, the goal, how it is played, and the audience targeted by this game):

1. List the cognitive skills derived from playing this game.

2. Do you think the content of the game influences the skills learned? If the video game you played had a very different content (for example, if it were more or less violent), would you still learn the same skills? Please explain.

3. Would the gender of the player influence the skills learned? Please explain.

4. What other characteristics of the player might influence the skills learned? Please explain.

5. Anthropologists and psychologists have studied how children's play activities develop competencies needed for adult roles. For example, Karen Watson-Gegeo and David Gegeo (1986) report that Kwar'ae children in the Solomon Islands learn appropriate adult language behaviors through the use of calling out routines during play. How might video games prepare young people to assume adult roles in your culture?

6. Would individuals who are not exposed to video games be deficient in skills needed to function as an adult in your culture? Please explain.

7. Describe at least one other cultural artifact (that is, a physical manifestation of culture) that prepares children to function as adults in your culture.

References:
   Greenfield, P. M. (1994). Video games as cultural artifacts. *Journal of Applied Developmental Psychology, 15*, 3-12.
   Nunes, T. (1995). Cultural practices and the conception of individual differences: Theoretical and empirical considerations. In J. J. Goodnow, P. J. Miller, & F. Kessel (Eds.), *Cultural practices as contexts for development: Vol. 67. New directions for child development* (pp. 91-104). San Francisco: Jossey-Bass.
   Schliemann, A. D., Carraher, D. W., & Ceci, S. J. (1997). Everyday cognition. In J. W. Berry, P. R. Dasen, & T. S. Saraswathi (Eds.), *Handbook of cross-cultural psychology: Vol. 2. Basic processes and human development* (2nd ed., pp. 177-216) Boston: Allyn & Bacon.
   Watson-Gegeo, K. A. & Gegeo, D. W. (1986). Calling out and repeating routines in Kwar'ae children's language socialization. In B. B. Schieffelin & E. Ochs (Eds.), *Language socialization across cultures* (pp. 17-50). Cambridge: Cambridge University Press.

Name _____   Date _____

Activity 3.6
CULTURE AND MEMORY STRATEGIES

The Laboratory of Comparative Human Cognition (1983) distinguished between two models of cognition: the central-processor model and the distributed-processor model. The central-processor model assumes that cognitive skills (such as perception, reasoning, and problem solving) develop and function in the same way regardless of context. According to the central-processor model, individuals would draw on these basic skills as needed regardless of the specific task at hand. The distributed-processor model, on the other hand, assumes that cognitive skills develop within the context of a specific task. According to the distributed-processor model, the form of the cognitive skill called upon will vary depending on the task. Rogoff and Mistry (1985) applied this distinction to the study of memory. They suggest that memory skills develop and function differently depending on the cultural context. This activity explores the cultural context of memory.

Directions: Complete each of the memory tasks below and answer the questions that follow.

1. Spend a minute memorizing the list of words below then cover the list with a sheet of paper and in the space to the right of the list, write down all the words that you remember.

- hammer
- envelope
- pen
- dish
- ink
- wrench
- screwdriver
- spoon
- eraser
- fork
- pliers
- paper

2. Describe the strategy you used to memorize the list of words.

3. In the space below, list the planets of the solar system.

4. Describe the strategy you originally used to memorize the planets.

5. In the space below, draw a map of your campus.

6. Describe the strategy you used to remember the layout of your campus.

7. Compare your map to a real map of your campus or to the maps of your classmates. What features did you emphasize or omit? Why?

8. Approximately how many phone numbers do you have committed to memory? Why have you not memorized the phone numbers of all of your family and friends?

9. Research on culture and memory has generally found that unschooled individuals do not perform as well as schooled individuals on tasks involving memorizing lists of words. What explanation can you provide for this finding?

10. Research on culture and memory has generally found that unschooled individuals may be quite skilled in memorizing large amounts of information such as family histories, star positions for navigating by sea, or agricultural facts. What explanation can you provide for this finding?

11. Based on this activity, what do you conclude about the validity of the central-processor versus the distributed-processor models? Please explain below.

References:

   Laboratory of Comparative Human Cognition (1983). Culture and cognitive development. In J. H. Flavell & E. M. Markman (Eds.), *Handbook of child psychology: Vol. III. Cognitive development.* New York: Wiley.

   Rogoff, B., & Mistry, J. (1985). Memory development in cultural context. In M. Pressley & C. Brainerd (Eds.), *The cognitive side of memory development.* New York: Springer-Verlag.

Name _____   Date _____

Activity 3.7
CULTURE AND AESTHETICS

A fascinating way to explore culture and perception is to examine aesthetic responses. Aesthetic responses have to do with whether one experiences perceiving something (such as artwork, music, poetry, or architecture) as pleasant, beautiful, attractive, or rewarding as opposed to unpleasant, ugly, unattractive or unrewarding (Russell, Deregowski, & Kinnear, 1997). By observing styles of art, music, architecture, and the like across cultures, we would quickly conclude that cultures vary markedly in what is deemed aesthetically pleasing. But are there any universal aspects of aesthetics that might be uncovered through cross-cultural research?

Berlyne (1960) proposed that several characteristics of a stimulus, called *collative variables*, may operate across cultures to determine aesthetic preferences. One of these collative variables is complexity. Several studies have found a relationship between the complexity of a stimulus and interest in or liking for that stimulus, although cultures may differ in the direction of the relationship. For example, Berlyne, Robbins, and Thompson (1974) reported that for participants from Canada, India, and Uganda, preference increased with complexity. Hekkert and van Wieringen (1990), however, found a curvilinear relationship between complexity and preference for non-representational abstract paintings (that is, preference was greatest for moderate levels of complexity) in studies in Holland. This activity explores the hypothesis that aesthetic preference is related to the complexity of the stimulus.

Directions: Create or locate three samples of the same type of stimulus that vary in complexity (for example, three musical phrases, photos of three different buildings, or a line of poetry from each of three different poems). One sample should be highly complex, one moderately complex, and one simple.

Identify 10 individuals to participate in this activity. Meet with each participant individually and ask him or her to rate the three items to indicate which they like most and like least. Record the responses on the data sheet below by putting a '1' in the blank to indicate 'most liked,' a '3' to indicate 'least liked', and a '2' to indicate the second-ranked stimulus. Once you have collected ratings of the three stimuli from each of your 10 participants, calculate the average rating for each level of complexity. Then answer the questions that follow.

Data Sheet

PARTICIPANT	LEVEL OF COMPLEXITY		
	LOW	MODERATE	HIGH
1			
2			
3			
4			
5			
6			
7			
8			
9			
10			
TOTAL SCORE			
AVERAGE SCORE			

Reactions:

1. Did your data support a relationship between level of complexity and aesthetic preference? If so, please explain the nature of that relationship.

2. If moderate levels of complexity are preferred across cultures, how might this be explained? (*Hint*: In trying to account for universal phenomena, psychologists typically first explore physiological explanations).

3. If you were to replicate this study with participants from markedly different cultures, what changes might you need to make in terms of the methods you used?

4. More recent research has focused on ecological variables (that have to do with the meaning and value of the stimulus) as predictors of aesthetic preferences. One of the better researched yet more controversial of these ecological variables is *prototypicality*, or the degree to which the stimulus is similar to the prototype -- or best example of -- a category. For example, when you think of the category "clothing" (depending upon the part of the world where you live) you may think of more prototypical items like "shirt" or "dress" before less prototypical items like "gloves" or "sweatshirt."

Look back at the three stimulus items you used for this activity. How would you rank them on prototypicality for their stimulus category (such as art, music, or architecture)? What do your data indicate about the relationship between aesthetic preference and prototypicality?

5. This activity has focused primarily on underlying *similarities* in aesthetic preferences across cultures. Describe below one factor that might help explain cultural *differences* in aesthetic preferences.

References:

Berlyne, D. E. (1960). *Conflict, arousal, and curiosity*. New York: McGraw-Hill.

Berlyne, D. E., Robbins, M. C., & Thompson, R. (1974). A cross-cultural study of exploratory and verbal responses to visual patterns varying in complexity. In D. E. Berlyne (Ed.), *Studies in the new experimental aesthetics* (pp. 259-278). New York: Wiley.

Hekkert, P., & van Wieringen, P. C. W. (1990). Complexity and prototypicality as determinants of the appraisal of paintings. *British Journal of Psychology, 81,* 483-495.

Russell, P. A., Deregowski, J. B., & Kinnear, P. R. (1997). Perception and aesthetics. In J. W. Berry, P. R. Dasen, & T. S. Saraswathi (Eds.), *Handbook of cross-cultural psychology: Vol 2. Basic processes and human development* (2nd ed., pp.107-142). Boston: Allyn & Bacon.

Name _____   Date _____

Activity 3.8
INTERPLANETARY PERCEPTION

This activity explores an experiment in interplanetary perception as a way to better understand the role of culture in shaping the way we perceive stimuli.

On March 3, 1972, *Pioneer 10*, the first spacecraft to leave our solar system, included a unique attempt to communicate with extraterrestrial life. The message took the form of a 6- by 9-inch gold anodized plaque that had been designed by astronomer Carl Sagan. It was hoped that the message might be intercepted by educated inhabitants of another star system who would be able to "read" its contents. As Gudykunst and Kim (1997) observed, the *Pioneer 10* plaque illustrates the nonverbal strategy typically taken when communication involves individuals who do not share a common language.

The components of the plaque (depicted below) are as follows:
1. The brackets indicate the height of the woman in comparison to the spacecraft. The man's arm is raised in a gesture of goodwill.
2. This figure represents a reverse in the direction of the spin of the electron in a hydrogen atom.
3. This represents the number 8 in binary form, indicating that the woman is 168 cm or 5'5" tall.
4. This radial pattern indicates the location of our solar system in the galaxy.
5. The shorter solid bars indicate directions to various pulsars from our sun and the periods of the pulsars in binary form, allowing the recipient to estimate the time the *Pioneer* was launched.
6. This indicates our solar system with the *Pioneer* originating from the Earth.

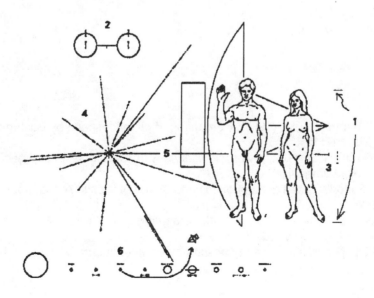

Directions: Examine the illustration of the *Pioneer 10* plaque above and read the description of its components. Then, in the space provided, draw on your knowledge of culture and perception to evaluate the likelihood that the plaque could effectively communicate with extraterrestrials. Below you will find two hints to start off your thinking on this matter.

Hint #1: A study by Winter (1963) explored the perception of safety posters by Bantu industrial workers. This study identified several instances in which the artist's symbolic meanings were not interpreted as intended, particularly when the perceiver was unschooled or from a rural area. For example, a red star intended as an indication that someone was hit was often thought to represent fire.

Hint #2: A significant number of cross-cultural studies have examined the perception of three-dimensional objects depicted in two dimensions (as in a photograph or drawing). The results of these studies (see, for example, Deregowski & Bentley, 1986; Hudson, 1960; McGurk & Jahoda, 1975) indicate that the ability to perceive depth varies greatly with educational background and the nature of the task.

Discuss below the likelihood that the plaque could effectively communicate with extraterrestrials:

References:
    Deregowski, J. B., & Bentley, A. M. (1986). Perception of pictorial space by Bushmen. *International Journal of Psychology, 21*, 51-119.
    Gudykunst, W. B., & Kim, Y. Y. (1997). *Communicating with strangers: An approach to intercultural communication.* New York: McGraw-Hill.
    Hudson, W. (1960). Pictorial depth perception in sub-cultural groups in Africa. *Journal of Social Psychology, 52*, 183-208.
    McGurk, H., & Jahoda, G. (1975). Pictorial depth perception by children in Scotland and Ghana. *Journal of Cross-Cultural Psychology, 6*, 279-296.
    Winter, W. (1963). The perception of safety posters by Bantu industrial workers. *Psychologia Africana, 10*, 127-135.

Name _____   Date _____

Activity 3.9
PHONETIC SYMBOLISM

This exercise will familiarize you with the phenomenon of phonetic symbolism. This term refers to the idea that speech sounds may themselves carry some universal meaning, regardless of the language in which they are found. Roger N. Brown, Abraham H. Black, and Arnold E. Horowitz (1955) suggested that speech may have its origins in symbols that somehow indicated their meaning and that remnants of these associations survive in existing languages. Though little research is currently conducted on phonetic symbolism, Edward Sapir's (1929) article on the topic was one of the earliest cross-cultural research reports to be published in a psychological journal.

Directions: For each of the word pairs, place the letter after the word with the corresponding English meaning. For example, for the first word pair in Mandarin, if you believe *mei* means beautiful and *ch'ou* means ugly, place a (b) next to *mei* and a (u) next to *ch'ou*. If you believe *ch'ou* means beautiful and *mei* means ugly, place a (b) next to *ch'ou* and a (u) next to *mei*. Of course, if you are familiar with any of the three languages then you should not complete the word pairs for those languages.

English	Mandarin	Czech	Hindi
1. beautiful (b)	mei	osklivost	badsurat
ugly (u)	ch'ou	krasa	khubsurat
2. blunt (b)	k'uai	tupy	tez
sharp (s)	tun	spicaty	gothil
3. bright (b)	liang	tmavy	chamakdar
dark (d)	an	svetly	drundhala
4. fast (f)	man	rychly	tez
slow (s)	k'uai	pomaly	sust
5. hard (h)	kang	mekky	sakht
soft (s)	jou	tvrdy	narm
6. light (l)	chung	tezky	wazani
heavy (h)	ch'ing	lehky	halka
7. warm (w)	nuan	teply	thanda
cool (c)	liang	chladny	garam

8. wide (w)   chai   siroky   chaura
   narrow (n)   k'uan   uzky   tang

Scoring: Check your responses against the answers on page 377. Circle all correct word pairs. The higher the number of correct choices, the stronger the evidence for phonetic symbolism (remember that by chance you would correctly identify 12 of the 24 word pairs).

Source:
   Adapted from Brown, R. N., Black, A. H., & Horowitz, A. E. (1955). Phonetic symbolism in four languages. *Journal of Abnormal and Social Psychology, 50,* 388-393.

Reference:
   Sapir, E. (1929). A study in phonetic symbolism. *Journal of Experimental Psychology, 12,* 225-239.

Name _____   Date _____

Activity 3.10
LINGUISTIC RELATIVITY

One of the earliest topics of cross-cultural research was the relationship between language and thought. Benjamin Whorf (1956) proposed that the structure of the language one speaks influences how one views the world. This concept has been called *linguistic relativity*. For example, Jamake Highwater (1981), suggested that English speakers and speakers of the Blackfeet Indian language see the world differently. He described how he was appalled to learn that English speakers use the word *wilderness* to describe the forest. From Highwater's Blackfeet Indian perspective, it is the cities that are wild and need taming rather than the forest, which is the natural state of the world.

A stronger version of this "Whorfian hypothesis" (also called the "Sapir-Whorf hypothesis" due to assistance Whorf received from linguist Edward Sapir) is that the language we speak *determines* the kinds of thoughts and perceptions we are capable of having. This idea is known as *linguistic determinism*. Many decades of linguistic, psychological, and anthropological research have provided conditional support for linguistic relativity in certain contexts (such as color-naming tasks). There has been less enthusiasm for the concept of linguistic determinism, although some research appears to support some aspects of linguistic determinism (Gumperz & Levinson, 1996). The complexity of the relationship between culture, language, and thought is the focus of this activity.

Jerry Dunn (1997) investigated the specialized terms used by subcultural groups such as Mountain Bike Riders, Disc Jockeys, Tabloid Reporters, Frisbee Players, and Science Fiction Fans. Dunn found Roller Coaster Enthusiasts use some of these terms:

- camel back -- a series of hills with each slightly smaller than the preceding one
- double dip -- a hill divided into two separate drops
- washboard -- a series of quick bumps as if one is rolling over a washboard

With these terms in mind, do you think you would perceive roller coasters differently (linguistic relativity)? Do you think you would have more difficulty perceiving these distinctions between roller coasters if you did not have these terms (linguistic determinism)? This activity explores the concepts of linguistic relativity and linguistic determinism and asks you to consider the validity of the Whorfian hypothesis.

Directions: This activity requires that you collect three terms used by a subculture of interest to you. You can find these terms by interviewing the members, exploring the websites, or reading the literature of a particular subculture. Once you have collected the three terms, respond to the questions below.

1. Describe the subculture that you investigated.

2. List the three subcultural terms and their definitions.

   a.

   b.

   c.

3. To what extent do you think having these terms would *influence* your thoughts or perceptions? Please explain.

4. To what extent do you think having these terms would *determine* your thoughts or perceptions? Please explain.

5. Hunt and Agnoli (1991) suggest that in some cases, language may not influence perception as much as it influences memory. Do you think you could remember the concepts represented by your terms better now that you have these terms in your vocabulary?

6. The empirical research findings on the Whorfian hypothesis are complex and address a wide variety of characteristics of language. Using your class readings, library resources, or an anthropology, psychology, or linguistics text, locate a description of research exploring the relationship between language and thought. Briefly summarize the research and its findings below. Be sure to cite your source(s).

7. How do your conclusions about language and thought correspond to the research findings you describe above?

References:

Dunn, J. (1997). *Idiom savant: Slang as it is slung.* New York: Henry Holt.

Gumperz, J. J., & Levinson, S. C. (1996). *Rethinking linguistic relativity.* Cambridge, England: Cambridge University Press.

Highwater, J. (1981). *The primal mind: Vision and reality in Indian America.* New York: HarperCollins.

Hunt, E., & Agnoli, F. (1991). The Whorfian hypothesis: A cognitive psychology perspective. *Psychological Review, 98*, 377-389.

Whorf, B. L. (1956). The relation of habitual thought and behavior to language. In J. B. Carroll (Ed.), *Language, thought, and reality: Selected writings of Benjamin Lee Whorf* (pp.134-159). Cambridge, MA: MIT Press.

Chapter 4. Culture and Developmental Processes

4.1 Parental Ethnotheories
4.2 Your Social Networks
4.3 Formal and Informal Learning
4.4 Home Culture and School Environment Fit
4.5 A Culturally Appropriate Piagetian Task
4.6 Culture and Perceptions of Growing Old
4.7 Culture and Gender Role Expectations
4.8 Peer Support of Academic Achievement
4.9 Ethnographic Studies of Human Development
4.10 Textbook Rewrite

Name _____   Date _____

Activity 4.1
PARENTAL ETHNOTHEORIES

Sara Harkness and Charles M. Super (1996) have written extensively on parents' cultural beliefs systems or what they term *parental ethnotheories*. Goodnow (1996) points out that there are several reasons why it is useful to study parents' cultural beliefs. These beliefs (1) provide insight into the cognition and development of adults, (2) help us understand parenting behavior, (3) are one aspect of the context in which children develop, and (4) when studied across generations, can provide clues about cultural transmission and change. This activity will allow you to explore a variety of parental ethnotheories and examine the cultural basis for your own beliefs about childrearing.

Directions: Circle the number to indicate your view on each of the parental ethnotheories below.

1. Everyone in the household has responsibility for keeping an eye on a crawling child or toddler.

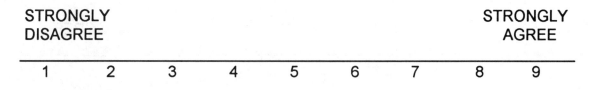

STRONGLY DISAGREE							STRONGLY AGREE	
1	2	3	4	5	6	7	8	9

2. Praising a child for accomplishing a task leads to disobedience and selfishness.

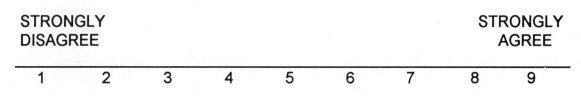

STRONGLY DISAGREE							STRONGLY AGREE	
1	2	3	4	5	6	7	8	9

3. It is cruel and neglectful to put a baby alone in a room to sleep.

STRONGLY DISAGREE							STRONGLY AGREE	
1	2	3	4	5	6	7	8	9

4. An infant is well cared for if he or she spends significant amounts of time being passed among many different adults, staying with no one person for more than several minutes at a time.

STRONGLY DISAGREE							STRONGLY AGREE	
1	2	3	4	5	6	7	8	9

5. Parents need to train their children in specific skills to prepare them for starting school.

STRONGLY DISAGREE							STRONGLY AGREE	
1	2	3	4	5	6	7	8	9

6. Babies should be encouraged to "sleep through the night" as soon as possible.

STRONGLY DISAGREE							STRONGLY AGREE	
1	2	3	4	5	6	7	8	9

7. Lactating women should freely nurse each other's children.

STRONGLY DISAGREE							STRONGLY AGREE	
1	2	3	4	5	6	7	8	9

8. Parents should respond immediately when their infant begins to cry.

STRONGLY DISAGREE							STRONGLY AGREE	
1	2	3	4	5	6	7	8	9

9. The role of parents is to protect and nurture their children, rather than stimulate their intellect.

STRONGLY DISAGREE								STRONGLY AGREE
1	2	3	4	5	6	7	8	9

10. Childhood tantrums are most likely due to a break in the child's daily routine.

STRONGLY DISAGREE								STRONGLY AGREE
1	2	3	4	5	6	7	8	9

11. It is important for babies' later development to receive verbal and visual stimulation.

STRONGLY DISAGREE								STRONGLY AGREE
1	2	3	4	5	6	7	8	9

12. By age 6 or 7 children are capable of caring for younger siblings.

STRONGLY DISAGREE								STRONGLY AGREE
1	2	3	4	5	6	7	8	9

13. A parent who doesn't use physical punishment doesn't fully love his or her child.

STRONGLY DISAGREE								STRONGLY AGREE
1	2	3	4	5	6	7	8	9

14. Parenting difficulties are best addressed by consulting medical or psychological experts or books written by such experts.

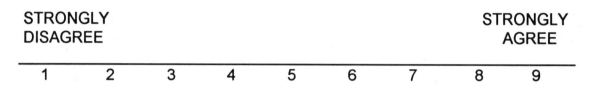

STRONGLY
DISAGREE

STRONGLY
AGREE

1   2   3   4   5   6   7   8   9

Reactions:

1. With which parental ethnotheory did you most strongly agree? Why?

2. With which parental ethnotheory did you most strongly disagree? Why?

3. Meredith Small (1998) includes an *eco-cultural* perspective (Berry, 1976) in her approach to understanding childrearing. She describes the many ways in which parenting beliefs and practices evolve in response to environmental as well as sociocultural demands. For example, she cites the case of the Ache of Paraguay who carry their children, rather than allowing them to crawl or walk - first in slings, then in baskets, and then piggyback -- until they are 5 years old. This practice makes sense considering the hazards for a small child crawling or walking in the forest environment of the Ache. How have the parental ethnotheories of your culture evolved in response to the physical or sociocultural environment? Please give an example below.

References:

    Berry, J. W. (1976). *Human ecology and cognitive style: Comparative studies in cultural and psychological adaptation*. New York: Sage/Halsted.

    Goodnow, J. J. (1996). From household practices to parents' ideas about work and interpersonal relationships. In S. Harkness & C. M. Super (Eds.), *Parents' cultural belief systems: Their origins, expressions, and consequences* (pp. 313-344). New York: Guilford.

    Harkness, S., & C. M. Super (1996). *Parents' cultural belief systems: Their origins, expressions, and consequences*. New York: Guilford.

    Small, M. F. (1998). *Our babies, ourselves: How biology and culture shape the way we parent*. New York: Anchor Books.

Name _____   Date _____

Activity 4.2
YOUR SOCIAL NETWORKS

Research on child development increasingly indicates the importance of social support in a child's emotional and social adjustment. Anne Marie Tietjen (1989) has discussed how children's support networks help them develop the skills they will need to be a competent adult within their own culture. For example, she compares the social network of an 8-year-old Swedish girl with that of a Maisin agemate in Papua New Guinea. She suggests that the Swedish child, who interacts with a variety of caregivers and teachers in addition to her nuclear family, gains competence in establishing relationships with previously unfamiliar people. The Maisin girl, who is in daily contact with her extended family, develops skills in maintaining long-term sources of support among kin. Anthropologist Thomas S. Weisner (1989) has observed that cultures may differ in what behaviors are perceived as supportive. For example, he reports that discussing a child's emotional reaction to events, a common form of social support among Americans, was virtually absent from the parent-child interactions he observed among the Abaluyia of Kenya. This activity will explore your own childhood support network and the competencies that developed as a result.

Directions: First think about your childhood social support network and make additions to the *types of social support* listed on the next page. Next, indicate with an 'X' on the chart that follows the source(s) of each type of social support listed. Finally, answer the questions that follow to examine the competencies that resulted from your social network.

Types of Social Support	SOURCES OF SOCIAL SUPPORT				
	Parents	Siblings	Extended Family	Nonfamily Adults	Nonfamily Children
Play					
Emotional Support/ Comfort					
Material Goods/ Services					
Positive Feedback/ Affection					
Advice/ Information					
Other:					
Other:					

Reactions:

1. For which types of social support were sources most available?

2. For which types of social support were sources least available?

3. In what ways did your social support network distinguish between the roles of children and adults?

4. What messages did you receive about gender roles from the structure of your social network?

5. Did your social network involve greater emphasis on short-term or long-term relationships? Please explain.

6. Did your social support system tend to encourage your independence from your family or interdependence with your family? Please explain.

References:
   Tietjen, A M. (1989). The ecology of children's social support networks. In D. Belle (Ed)., *Children's social networks and social supports* (pp. 37-69). New York: Wiley.
   Weisner, T. S. (1989). Cultural and universal aspects of social support for children: Evidence from the Abaluyia of Kenya. In D. Belle (Ed.), *Children's social networks and social supports* (pp. 70-90). New York: Wiley.

Name _____   Date _____

Activity 4.3
FORMAL AND INFORMAL LEARNING

Psychologists and anthropologists have studied the different processes involved in informal education (that occurs in the course of day-to-day activities) and formal (school-based) teaching. For example, learning how to be humorous or how to ride a bicycle might be taught informally whereas learning mathematical skills or historical dates may be taught through formal schooling. Researchers have identified various effects of schooling on cognitive development. For example, schooled children are more likely to solve problems by extracting general rules whereas unschooled children tend to solve problems singly (Scribner & Cole, 1973). More recently, educators have focused on ways to make the typical classroom more welcoming of people with diverse backgrounds by integrating some of the qualities of informal learning into formal education. The purpose of this activity is to explore some of the differences between formal and informal education.

Directions: List five skills that you learned through formal education and five skills that you learned through informal means. Then answer the questions that follow to compare these two forms of learning.

Formal Education
1.

2.

3.

4.

5.

Informal Education
1.

2.

3.

4.

5.

1. For each of the following statements, indicate by marking the appropriate blank with an 'X' whether they are more true of formal or informal education.

	Formal	Informal
a. Learning occurs in a specified setting and time period.	_____	_____
b. Learning occurs through observation.	_____	_____
c. Emotions are kept separate from the subject matter.	_____	_____
d. The teacher has a personal connection with the subject matter.	_____	_____
e. Teachers of a specific subject are basically interchangeable.	_____	_____
f. Cooperation more than competition characterizes the interaction among learners.	_____	_____
g. The subject matter is closely tied to life experiences.	_____	_____
h. The learning process is fairly structured and predictable.	_____	_____

2. What difficulties might arise for someone from a culture that depends heavily on informal education if they were to enter a formal schooling situation?

3. What characteristics of informal learning might be helpful to integrate into a formal educational setting?

4. Robert Serpell and Giyoo Hatano (1997) have described how reading skills can be acquired outside of a school setting. What other skills that are typically taught in school might also be learned through informal means?

References:

Scribner, S., & Cole, M. (1973). Cognitive consequences of formal and informal education. *Science, 182*, 553-559.

Serpell, R., & Hatano, G. (1997). Education, schooling, and literacy. In J. W. Berry, P. R. Dasen, & T. S. Saraswathi (Eds.), *Handbook of cross-cultural psychology: Vol. 2. Basic processes and human development* (2nd ed., pp. 339-376). Boston: Allyn & Bacon.

Name _____   Date _____

Activity 4.4
HOME CULTURE AND SCHOOL ENVIRONMENT FIT

This exercise will examine the importance of the fit between home culture and school environment for the academic success and well-being of children.

Directions: Read the information below and respond to the questions in the space provided.

1. Statistics show that children of Hawaiian ancestry, particularly those from low-income families, tend to be academic underachievers. In addition, they may be stereotyped by their teachers as lazy, uncooperative, and disinterested.

What would you predict about the home life of these children?

2. According to Jordon and colleagues (1992) the behavior of Hawaiian children at home stands in sharp contrast to the perceptions of their teachers. These authors suggest that the following characteristics describe many Hawaiian families:

- Very young children make significant contributions to household work.

- Siblings work cooperatively to complete tasks.

- Parents may indicate a task to be done, but the children will determine how it is to be accomplished and by whom.

- Older children may supervise the work of younger children.

- Children learn through observation and imitation.

- Children determine for themselves when they are able to take on tasks that are more complex or require greater responsibility.

- Values emphasize contributing to the well-being of the family as a unit.

- Helping each other and working together symbolizes close family ties.

Does this description correspond to your answer to question 1? Why or why not?

3. Think about the typical classroom in many parts of the world. The teacher stands in the front of the class and is in control of all that occurs within the classroom walls. The teacher sets out class rules, assigns and supervises tasks, and determines how resources are used and allocated.

Discuss the fit between the home culture and school environment for children of Hawaiian ancestry. Be specific in terms of the skills required for, and values characteristic of, each setting.

4. How might you explain the poor academic performance of Hawaiian children and the perceptions of the teachers that they are lazy, disinterested, and uncooperative?

5. Describe a school environment one might design to better fit the home culture of Hawaiian children. Be sure to discuss the role of teachers, peer interaction, "ownership" of the classroom, teaching style, and classroom values.

6. Hawaii's Kamehameha Early Education Program (KEEP) demonstrates that the school environment can be successfully modified to increase compatibility with home culture and thus increase academic achievement (Jordon, Tharp, & Baird-Vogt, 1992). Think about the fit between your own home culture and the school environment where your education took place. To what extent were they compatible? What changes might have been made to your classroom to make it more compatible with your home culture?

Source:
     Based on Jordon, C., Tharp, R., & Baird-Vogt, L. (1992). Just open the door: Cultural compatibility and classroom rapport. In M. Saravia-Shore & S. Arivizu (Eds.), *Cross-cultural literacy: Ethnographies of communication in multiethnic classrooms* (pp. 3-18). New York: Garland.

Name _____   Date _____

Activity 4.5
A CULTURALLY APPROPRIATE PIAGETIAN TASK

Early cross-cultural studies of cognitive abilities often found deficiencies in the mental abilities of individuals from less industrialized societies. Later studies of this type demonstrate, however, that these individuals' *performance* on cognitive tasks did not likely indicate their level of *competence*. One of the reasons for this was that the earlier studies tended to use materials that were not familiar to the participants. An interesting study by Irwin, Schafer, and Feiden (1974) demonstrates the importance of familiarity of task materials. In this study, nonliterate Liberian adults and American college students were asked to perform two sorting tasks. One task involved sorting geometric figures differing in color, shape, and number. The second task involved sorting bowls of rice that differed in size of bowl, type of rice, and cleanness of the grains. The Americans performed better than the Liberians on the geometric figures task, whereas the Liberians performed better than the Americans on the rice sorting task. Each group performed better on the task that utilized familiar materials.

A large number of cross-cultural studies of cognitive development have focused on Piagetian tasks. Jean Piaget's theory of cognitive development specifies a distinct structure of thought that differs at each of four stages of development. Cross-cultural research supports the sequence of stages described by Piaget, though the ages at which different stages are attained varies across cultures (Dasen & Heron, 1981). Children performing tasks with familiar materials were more likely than those using unfamiliar materials to demonstrate mastery of the thought structure of the stage assessed (Price-Williams, 1981). The purpose of this activity is to think about how one might develop a culturally appropriate Piagetian task.

Directions: Use an introductory psychology textbook to review the concept of Piagetian conservation. Then devise a task to test conservation of quantity, mass, or number. This task should be appropriate for children in a specific culture with which you are familiar. Use materials for this task that are commonly found in the culture you selected. For example, Geoffrey Saxe and Thomas Moylan (1982) developed a Piagetian conservation task appropriate for the Oksapmin of Papua New Guinea. The task involved the measurement of string bags, a commonly used object in Oksapmin culture and required that people understand that the length of bags remains constant regardless of whether it is measured along the arm of a child or the arm of an adult.

In the spaces provided below, indicate the culture and conservation task you have selected and then describe the task and materials used.

1. The task below is intended to measure conservation of _____ for members of the _____ culture.

2. Description of the task and materials:

References:

Dasen, P. R., & Heron, A. (1981). Cross-cultural tests of Piaget's theory. In H. C. Triandis & A. Heron (Eds.), *Handbook of cross-cultural psychology: Vol. 4. Developmental psychology* (pp. 295-341). Boston: Allyn & Bacon.

Irwin, M. H., Schafer, G. N., & Feiden, C. P. (1974). Emic and unfamiliar category sorting of Mano farmers and U.S. undergraduates. *Journal of Cross-Cultural Psychology, 5,* 407-423.

Price-Williams, D. (1981). Concrete and formal operations. In R. H. Munroe, R. L. Monroe, & B. D. Whiting (Eds.), *Handbook of cross-cultural human development* (pp. 403-422). New York: Garland Press.

Saxe, G. B., & Moylan, T. (1982). The development of measurement operations among the Oksapmin of Papua New Guinea. *Child Development, 53,* 1242-1248.

Name _____   Date _____

Activity 4.6
CULTURE AND PERCEPTIONS OF GROWING OLD

With medical advances increasing life expectancies throughout the world, our perceptions of old age become important to examine. Deborah Best and John Williams (1996) note that stereotypes of the elderly are unlike other stereotypes in that they involve perceptions of a group of which we all expect to be a member. These authors conducted a study of young adults' views of growing old in 19 different countries on six continents: Africa (South Africa, Zimbabwe), Asia (India, Korea, Malaysia, Pakistan, Turkey), Europe (Finland, Germany, Norway, Poland, Portugal, Wales), North America (Canada, the USA), Oceania (New Zealand), and South America (Chile, Peru, Venezuela). The purpose of this activity is to assess your own views of growing old and compare them to the cross-cultural data reported by Best and Williams.

Directions: Please respond to the questions below. The Attitude Toward Aging items have been adapted from the questionnaire used in Best and Williams' research.

Attitudes Toward Aging

1. When you hear someone described as being "old," what age do you think of? At least _____ years of age.

2. When you hear someone described as being "middle aged," what age do you think of? At least _____ years of age.

3. Put an 'X' next to the decade that you expect to be the most satisfying and productive years of *your* life.

_____ 0-9 years	_____ 40-49 years	_____ 70-79 years
_____ 10-19 years	_____ 50-59 years	_____ 80-89 years
_____ 20-29 years	_____ 60-69 years	_____ 90-99 years
_____ 30-39 years		

4. Overall, how do you feel about growing older (circle the number below that indicates your answer).

Very _____ Very
Negatively   1   2   3   4   5   6   Positively

Reactions: In answering the questions below, compare your answer to the Attitudes Toward Aging items to Best and Williams' findings.

1. On the average across the 19 countries, "old" was described by males as being at least 60 years and by females as being at least 62 years of age. Malaysian females gave the lowest minimum age for being old (53.9 years) and Portuguese females gave the highest minimum age for being old (67.9 years). Considering these results and your own response, what factors do you think contribute to one's view of the age one becomes "old"?

2. On the average across the 19 countries, "middle aged" was described by males as being at least 39 years and by females as being at least 41 years of age. Malaysian males gave the lowest minimum age for being middle aged (35.1 years) and Portuguese females gave the highest minimum age for being middle aged (47.8 years). Considering these results and your own response, what factors do you think contribute to one's view of the age one becomes "middle aged"?

3. Across the 19 countries both males and females thought their 20s and 30s would be the most satisfying and productive time of their lives. Women in more developed countries indicated somewhat later ages as being the best time in their lives. Considering these results and your own response, what factors do you think contributes to one's expectancies about the period of life that will be most satisfying or productive?

4. Across the 19 countries, both males and females gave an overall rating of growing older that was neutral (3.72 on a 6-point scale). Participants from Venezuela and from Chile gave the most positive ratings of growing old, whereas the participants from Pakistan, Canada, and Zimbabwe gave the most negative ratings. The overall ratings of growing older were not related to measures of economic development or to actual life expectancies. Considering these results and your own response, what factors do you think contributes to one's overall rating of growing old?

5. How might perceptions of growing older, such as those measured in this study, influence social policy (for example, the funding of services for the elderly)?

6. Do you think young adults' perceptions of growing old are accurate or inaccurate? Might perceptions of growing older be more accurate in some cultures than others? Please explain.

7. Do you think efforts should be made to change young adults' perceptions of growing older? Why or why not?

Source:

The Attitudes Toward Aging items were adapted from Best, D. L., & Williams, J. E. (1996). Anticipation of aging: A cross-cultural examination of young adults' views of growing old. In J. Pandey, D. Sinha, & D. P. S. Bhawuk (Eds.), *Asian contributions to cross-cultural psychology* (pp. 274-288). These items first appeared in Osteen, F. L. (1985). Aspects of subjective age and their relationship to physical, mental, and emotional well being. Unpublished master's thesis. Wake Forest University.

Name _____   Date _____

Activity 4.7
CULTURE AND GENDER ROLE EXPECTATIONS

An important aspect of culture is expectations about gender-based behaviors and attributes. This activity uses a content analysis of magazine advertisements in order to explore culture and gender role expectations.

Directions: Select two recent magazines, one targeted to men and one targeted to women (avoid purely fashion magazines). Carefully read the descriptions of coding categories and then, using the coding sheet provided, tally the number of advertisements that fall under each category. Note any additional findings of interest that may not be reflected by the number of advertisements. For example, you may find the same number of car advertisements in both men's and women's magazines, but may find more sports cars in the men's magazines and more minivans in the women's magazines. Once you have coded your data, respond to the questions that follow.

Coding Categories:
Alcohol -- Such as beer, wine, liquor, or any alcoholic beverage or beverage mix.

Apparel -- Such as clothes, shoes (except sports shoes), glasses, watches, jewelry, belts, ties, handbags, and wallets.

Automotive -- Such as cars, trucks, car repair services.

Beauty and Personal Care -- Such as cosmetics, hair products, skin lotions or cleansers, deodorants, toothpastes, feminine hygiene products, cologne/perfume, and breath fresheners.

Child and Baby Care -- Such as diapers, baby food, children's toys, books, or music.

Cleaning -- Household cleaning products such as laundry detergent, furniture polish, dishwashing liquid, floor cleaner, glass cleaner, or disinfectants.

Crafts and Collectibles -- Including hobby-related products, and collectible dolls, dishes, or figurines.

Electronic Products -- Such as computers and software, fax machines, pagers, phones, televisions, video or stereo equipment.

Financial Services -- Such as banking or brokerage services, tax preparation services, or financial consulting services.

Food and (Nonalcoholic) Beverages -- Any food or (nonalcoholic) drink in a prepared or natural state including mixes, canned, or frozen products, bottled water, candy, or gum.

Home Renovation -- Such as furniture, appliances, house paint, flooring, or fixtures.

Medications and Vitamins -- Such as pain relievers, antacids, laxatives, contraceptives, antidepressants, vitamins, weight control products, or nutritional supplements.

Sports and Outdoor Equipment -- Such as exercise equipment, bicycles, roller blades, gym bags, or sports shoes.

Tobacco Products -- Such as cigarettes, cigars, or chewing tobacco.

Magazine Coding Sheet

PRODUCT	WOMEN'S MAGAZINE	MEN'S MAGAZINE
Alcohol		
Apparel		
Automotive		
Beauty & Personal Care		
Child & Baby Care		
Cleaning		
Crafts & Collectibles		
Electronic Equipment		
Financial Services		
Food & (Nonalcoholic) Beverages		
Home Renovation		
Medications & Vitamins		
Sports & Outdoor		
Tobacco		

Reactions:

1. Based on the data you collected, describe below the cultural expectations of women and of men as depicted in the magazine advertisements.

2. To what extent do you believe these messages shape gender-typed behavior? Are these messages primarily reinforced or contradicted elsewhere in the culture? Please explain.

3. John Williams and Deborah Best (1990) found a great deal of consensus across cultures in the attributes associated with males and females. In a study of sex role stereotypes involving 30 different countries, being female in these countries was associated with, for example, being attractive, dependent, emotional, sensitive, and weak whereas being male was associated with being adventurous, dominant, independent, and strong. Did you find any indications of these attributes in the magazine ads you examined? If so, please give an example.

Reference:
Williams, J., & Best, D. (1990). *Measuring sex stereotypes: A thirty-nation study* (rev. ed.). Newbury Park, CA: Sage.

Name _____   Date _____

Activity 4.8
PEER SUPPORT OF ACADEMIC ACHIEVEMENT

Research has found ethnic differences in academic achievement. For example, studies in the United States consistently find that *on the average*, Asian American students outperform students from other ethnic groups. Several explanations for such findings have been proposed, the least well supported of which is that there are genetic differences between ethnic groups associated with intellectual abilities. More useful explanations have focused on the impact of discrimination, ethnic differences in socialization for achievement, and cultural values associated with education. Studies by Steinberg, Dornbusch, and Brown (1992) point to an additional component involved in ethnic differences in academic achievement -- the role of peers. They suggest that a critical predictor of academic success in adolescence is having support for academics *both* from parents and peers. Andrew Fuligni (1997) reported that support from parents and peers also predicted the academic achievement of students from immigrant families in the United States. This activity involves conducting an interview in order to explore the role of peer support in academic achievement.

Directions:
Select a respondent. For this activity you will need to recruit a college student to respond to a series of interview questions.

Check for time constraints. Reserve at least 30 minutes for the interview.

Obtain informed consent. Explain the purpose of the interview (to explore influences on academic achievement) and be sure that your respondent understands that his or her responses may be discussed in class or included in a written report.

Assure and maintain confidentiality. Be sure you tell your respondent that you will not in any way attach his or her name to the responses in reporting or discussing the responses to the interview. It is critical that you maintain this confidentiality in order to conduct the interview in an ethical manner.

Conduct the interview. Ask the interview questions in the order in which they appear in this activity. Be sure to take notes in the space provided or on a separate sheet.

Summarize the interview data for each respondent and then complete the reactions section of this activity.

Provide feedback to the respondent if appropriate. If you have some general conclusions about influences on academic achievement based on discussing or analyzing the interview data with your class, you might convey these conclusions to your respondent. Be sure to thank him or her for the time spent assisting you with this activity.

Describe your respondent: Include gender, age, level in school, parents' education level, and ethnic/racial identity (you may need to ask your respondent for some of this information).

Interview questions:

1. What messages did you receive from your family about academics?

2. Did your parents or other family members do anything in particular that indicated their views about education?

3. What messages did you receive about the impact of getting a good education on your later job opportunities?

4. How would you describe your primary peer group in high school?

5. To what extent did you have a choice of peer groups in high school?

6. What was the attitude of most of your peers about academics? Did you feel you could be popular with your peers and do well in school at the same time?

7. Did you spend much time studying or discussing assignments with your friends?

8. To what do you attribute your current attitudes about academic achievement?

Summary: Summarize your findings by discussing the factors that appear to have played a role in the academic achievement of your interviewee.

Reactions:

Below are some of the findings from Steinberg, Dornbusch, and Brown's study. (Keep in mind that along with differences *between* ethnic groups there is generally much variability *within* ethnic groups.) Please read the findings below and then answer the questions that follow.

- Whereas parents had a greater influence on students' long-term educational goals, peers had a greater influence on day-to-day behaviors in school (such as attendance rates, classroom behavior, and time spent on homework). Steinberg and colleagues' data indicates that across ethnic groups, students who had both parental and peer support for academics had the highest level of academic success.

- Peer support for academics often involved belonging to a peer group in which students study together and help each other with difficult assignments.

- Students had higher levels of academic achievement if they were fearful that doing poorly in school would have negative consequences. (Asian American students were generally more concerned about the negative consequences of academic failure than students from other ethnic groups.)

1. Discuss the degree to which your interview data supports Steinberg and colleagues' findings.

2. Based on your interview data, construct a research question for future study of ethnicity and academic achievement.

References:

Fuligni, A. J. (1997). The academic achievement of adolescents from immigrant families: The roles of family background, attitudes, and behavior. *Child Development, 68,* 351-363.

Steinberg, L., Dornbusch, S. M., & Brown, B. B. (1992). Ethnic differences in academic achievement: An ecological perspective. *American Psychologist, 47,* 723-729.

Name _____   Date _____

Activity 4.9
ETHNOGRAPHIC STUDIES OF HUMAN DEVELOPMENT

Thomas S. Weisner (1996) has argued that ethnography is the most important method of studying human development. Ethnography involves recording observations of daily behavior, generally over an extended period of time. Ethnographic researchers typically take very in-depth notes on their observations and may work with knowledgeable members of the community they are studying (sometimes called *informants*). At times ethnographic researchers even take part in the activities they are studying, a technique called *participant observation*.

In a research technique called the *hologeistic* method, hypotheses are tested using collections of ethnographies. One of the most widely used collections of ethnographic research is the Human Relations Area Files (HRAF). The HRAF contains ethnographies from over 360 societies. In hologeistic research, societies rather than individuals are used as the unit of analysis (yielding what has been called *ecological correlations*). For example, in a classic study by Barry, Child, and Bacon (1959), data from the HRAF confirmed the hypothesis that high food accumulating societies would use socialization practices that endorse compliance rather than independence.

The following studies are examples of ethnographic research.

- Pierrette Hondagneu-Sotelo and Ernestine Avila (1997) have written an ethnography on what they call the "transnational motherhood" of Latina immigrant women who work as nannies or housekeepers in Los Angeles while their own children remain in their countries of origin.

- An ethnographic study of Sicilian Canadian older adults conducted by Sam Migliore (1993) examined how the metaphor of "nerves" is used to communicate social and emotional distress.

- Robin L. Jarrett's (1997) ethnography of urban African American families explored how parents in difficult socioeconomic circumstances are able to generate self-esteem and self-efficacy in their children.

The purpose of this activity is to become familiar with the method of ethnography, particularly as it informs our understanding of human development.

Directions: Using library resources, locate an ethnography addressing some aspect of human development. Such studies focus on understanding the context of experiences and adaptations throughout the lifespan. The research article you select should describe a study conducted in a culture other than your own. Many social science books and journals include ethnographies. However, some particularly good sources for ethnographic accounts include:

American Ethnologist	Gender and Society
Contemporary Sociology	Human Ecology
Cultural Anthropology	Journal of Aging Studies
Culture	Journal of Black Studies
Culture, Medicine, and Psychiatry	Journal of Comparative Family Studies
Ethos	Journal of Contemporary Ethnography

After carefully reading your ethnography, answer the questions below. Be sure to attach a photocopy of your article to this worksheet.

1. In the space below, provide the full citation for your article (see the reference section of activities in this book for examples of the format and content of citations).

2. Describe the purpose of this ethnographic study.

3. Describe the ethnographic methods that were involved in this study.

4. Summarize the findings of the study. In what way did this research contribute to our understanding of human development?

5. What do you think might be some strengths and weaknesses of the ethnographic approach?

References:
   Barry, H. III, Child, I. L., & Bacon, M. K. (1959). Relation of child training to subsistence economy. *American Anthropologist, 61,* 51-63.

   Hondagneu-Sotelo, P., & Avila, E. (1997). "I'm here, but I'm there": The meanings of Latina transnational motherhood. *Gender and Society, 11,* 548-571.

   Jarrett, R. L. (1997). Resilience among low-income African American youth: An ethnographic perspective. *Ethos, 25,* 218-229.

   Migliore, S. (1993). "Nerves": The role of metaphor in the cultural framing of experience. *Journal of Contemporary Ethnography, 22,* 331-360.

   Weisner, T. S. (1996) Why ethnography should be the most important method in the study of human development. In R. Jessor & S. Colby (Eds.), *Ethnography and human development: Context and meaning in social inquiry* (pp. 305-324). Chicago: University of Chicago Press.

Name _____   Date _____

Activity 4.10
TEXTBOOK REWRITE

As you learn more about culture and psychology you may find that you view your psychology lectures and reading materials from a new perspective. In fact, you may be tempted to fill in information about cultural variability or modify existing information to be more inclusive of diverse populations. This activity gives you an opportunity to do just that.

Directions: Select a 3 to 5-paragraph segment of a developmental psychology textbook or the developmental chapter of an introductory psychology textbook. Rewrite the material so that it is more inclusive of research addressing the influence of culture.

1. Use library resources or cross-cultural texts to locate material on the influence of culture on socialization and developmental processes.

2. Make the appropriate citations for the material you include (see References in this book for examples of citation format).

3. Attach a copy of the original textbook passages and your rewrite to this sheet.

4. The task of this activity is not just a matter of adding information to the existing working of the text, but will require some significant rewriting so as not to *marginalize* the material on culture.   Information on cultural factors that appears in the "boxes" of texts, or in a separate diversity chapter, may convey the message that culture is not central to an understanding of human behavior and may portray members of various cultural groups as exotic "others" to be contrasted with what is portrayed as typical or normal. An example of an inclusive rewrite that does not marginalize diverse perspectives is provided below.

Original:
> Baumrind's (1971) research indicates that parents generally employ one of three socialization patterns: authoritarian, permissive, or authoritative socialization.

Cultural influences included but marginalized:
> Baumrind's (1971) research indicates that parents generally employ one of three socialization patterns: authoritarian, permissive, or authoritative socialization. However, these patterns may not apply to all ethnic groups.

Inclusive rewrite:

> Research focusing on members of nuclear families, such as Baumrind's (1971) study of European American parents, has identified three main socialization patterns: authoritarian, permissive, or authoritative parenting. Studies addressing extended families, such as Chao's (1994) study of Chinese Americans, have found parenting styles that emphasize training children to know what is expected of them.

In the space below provide the complete citation for the textbook you have selected.

References:

Baumrind, D. (1971). Current patterns of parental authority. *Developmental Psychology Monographs, 4*(1, part 2).

Chao, R. K. (1994). Beyond parental control and authoritarian parenting style: Understanding Chinese parenting through the cultural notion of training. *Child Development, 65*, 1111-1119.

Chapter 5. Personality, Emotion, and the Self in Cultural context

Name _____   Date _____

Activity 5.1
THE INTERDEPENDENT AND INDEPENDENT SELVES

This activity focuses on a key distinction between cultures, whether the self is viewed as interdependent or independent (Markus & Kitayama, 1991). Collectivist cultures have been associated with a self-system that is inseparable from the social context. In other words, the self is defined in terms of relationships. The independent self, more typical of individualistic cultures, focuses on individual traits, abilities, goals, and preferences. The degree to which we hold an interdependent versus independent self-construal may impact how we process thoughts, how we experience and express our emotions, and how and when we are motivated.

Directions: Read each of the items in the two columns below and place a check next to the item in each pair that best describes you.

_____ Success depends on help from others.	_____ Success depends on my abilities.
_____ I know more about others than I do about myself.	_____ I know more about myself than I do about others.
_____ Being excluded from my group would be very hard on me.	_____ Being dependent on others would be very hard on me.
_____ Silence is comfortable.	_____ Silence is embarrassing.
_____ It is important that my behavior is appropriate for the situation.	_____ It is important that my behavior and attitudes correspond.
_____ I sometimes feel ashamed.	_____ I sometimes feel guilty.
_____ Friendships are difficult to establish, but are generally very intimate.	_____ Friendships are fairly easy to establish, but often not very intimate.
_____ I generally socialize in groups.	_____ I generally socialize in pairs.
_____ **Total number of checks**	_____ **Total number of checks**

Reactions:

1. The items in the column on the left indicate characteristics of the interdependent self whereas items in the column on the right indicate characteristics of the independent self. According to the total number of checks for each column, is your self-construal more interdependent or independent? To what extent does your cultural background explain this result?

2. Harry Triandis (1994) suggests that we may have both interdependent and independent aspects of self. Which one we draw from at any given moment may depend on our cultural experiences and the situation. Describe below an instance in which you acted from an interdependent self-contrual and one in which you acted from an independent self-construal.

3. Susan Cross and Laura Madson (1997) suggest in their research review that women in the United States tend to maintain a more interdependent self-construal whereas men tend to maintain a more independent self-construal. To what extent to you think your gender affected your responses to the checklists?

4. Theodore Singelis (1995) reported greater embarrassability among research participants with interdependent self-construals than independent self-construals. Based on what you have learned about these two self-systems, how might you explain this finding?

5. Based on what you have learned about interdependent and independent self-construals, what would you predict about the communication styles of people with these two self-systems?

References:
Cross, S. E., & Madson, L. (1997). Models of the self: Self-construals and gender. *Psychological Bulletin, 122,* 5-37.
Markus, H., & Kitayama, S. (1991). Culture and self: Implications for cognition, emotion and motivation. *Psychological Review, 98,* 224-253.
Singelis, T. M. (1995).Culture, self-construal, and embarrassability. *Journal of Cross-Cultural Psychology, 26,* 622-644.
Triandis, H. C. (1994). *Culture and social psychology.* New York: McGraw-Hill.

Name _____ Date _____

Activity 5.2
COLLECTIVE SELF-ESTEEM

Most students of psychology have read something about the concept of self-esteem and the role self-esteem plays in self-concept and well-being, but are there other forms of self-esteem in addition to our appraisal of ourselves as individuals? Jennifer Crocker and Riia Luhtanen (1990) have identified another facet of our self-esteem derived from our membership in various groups, such as those based on race, gender, and religion. They call this *collective self-esteem*. This activity is designed to provide you with a way to explore your own collective self-esteem and to think critically about this concept.

Directions: Before answering the questions below, think for a moment about the different social groups to which you belong. These include such categories as gender, race, ethnicity, social class, nationality, occupation and many others. Choose just one social group to focus on for this activity.

Write the name of the group here: _____

1. (*Membership Component*) To what extent do you feel that you make a worthwhile contribution to this social group? Why?

2. (*Private Component*) To what extent are you satisfied with being a member of this social group? Why?

3. (*Public Component*) To what extent do you feel this social group is valued and respected by others? Why?

4. (*Identity Component*) To what extent is belonging to this social group an important part of your identity? Why?

5. Reread your answers to the four questions above, which represent Luhtanen and Crocker's (1992) four components of collective self-esteem (Membership, Private, Public, and Identity, respectively). Using the levels below, rate your answers for the amount of collective self-esteem indicated.

Component	Level of Collective Self-Esteem		
Membership	Low	Moderate	High
Private	Low	Moderate	High
Public	Low	Moderate	High
Identity	Low	Moderate	High

Lutanen and Crocker raise several interesting questions regarding collective self-esteem and its four components. Based on your responses to the four components, think about and respond to the issues below:

1. What are some of factors that might impact the development of collective self-esteem?

2. How would you describe the relationship between personal self-esteem and collective self-esteem?

3. Is collective self-esteem a stable personality trait (that is, is it likely to be consistent across time and situations) or is it a temporary state?

4. What do think might be the impact of collective self-esteem on psychological adjustment and well-being?

5. Think about how collective self-esteem might be used as a variable in research on psychology and culture. Write a research hypothesis involving collective self-esteem in the form of a sentence below.

6. Can you think of some other aspects of collective self-esteem other than the four above? If so, what are they?

Source:

   Items based on Luhtanen, R., & Crocker, J. A collective self-esteem scale: Self-evaluation of one's social identity. *Personality and Social Psychology Bulletin, 18*, 302-318. Copyright (c) 1992 by Sage Publications, Inc. Adapted with permission.

Reference:

   Crocker, J., & Luhtanen, R. (1990). Collective self-esteem and ingroup bias. *Journal of Personality and Social Psychology, 58*, 60-67.

Name _____   Date _____

Activity 5.3
BIRACIAL IDENTITY

Beverly Tatum (1997, p. 168) uses the term "biracial baby boom" to refer to marked increases in the rate of biracial children in the United States; a rate that has tripled over the past two decades. Maria Root (1998) has conducted extensive research on the racial/ethnic identity of biracial individuals. Some of her observations include the following:

- Individuals of mixed race/ethnicity are increasingly likely to identify themselves as racially/ethnically mixed.

- Racial/ethnic appearance does not predict racial/ethnic identity.

- An individual's racial/ethnic identity may change over time and across situations.

- Siblings of the same mixed heritage may have different racial/ethnic identities.

This activity deals with the many factors that influence racial/ethnic identity among biracial individuals.

Directions: Please respond to each of the questions below in the space provided.

1. Imagine that you are the child of an Asian mother and a Black father. Describe your likely ethnic/racial identity.

2. Describe how this racial/ethnic identity might change under the following conditions:

  a. You live with your father only.

  b. You live with your mother only.

c. Your appearance is of a Black person.

d. Your appearance is of an Asian person.

e. Your appearance is racially ambiguous.

f. You live in a predominantly Black neighborhood and have mostly Black friends.

g. You live in a predominantly Asian neighborhood and have mostly Asian friends.

h. You live in a racially mixed neighborhood and have friends from different ethnic and racial groups.

i. Your parents encourage knowledge of your ethnic and racial heritage.

j. Your parents rarely discuss issues of race or ethnicity.

k. Your family has experienced some acts of discrimination due to their interracial makeup.

l. Your family has never experienced any discrimination.

m. You are male.

n. You are female.

3. Discuss the relative importance of the factors listed above in terms of their contribution to ethnic/racial identity.

4. What other factors do you think might be relevant?

References:
Root, M. P. P. (1998). Experiences and processes affecting racial identity development: Preliminary results from the biracial sibling project. *Cultural Diversity and Ethnic Minority Psychology, 4,* 237-247.
Tatum, B. D. (1997).*"Why are all the Black kids sitting together in the cafeteria?" And other conversations about race.* New York: Basic Books.

Name _____   Date _____

Activity 5.4
NICKNAMING ACROSS CULTURES

Researchers from a wide variety of disciplines have studied nicknames as a means to better understand the origin and change in patterns of culture. For example, a study of nicknames used by the Warlpiri in the Northern Territory of Australia indicates that nicknames may reinforce Warlpiri values by deriding people who deviate from Warlpiri ways (Nicholls, 1995). Nicknames have also been studied in order to understand cultural change. For example, Jack Glazier (1987), an anthropologist, found that the use of nicknames by community members has decreased along with suburbanization in the American Midwest. The purpose of this activity is to explore how nicknames may be used to reinforce cultural values.

Directions:

Select three interviewees. Identify three individuals who have been nicknamed and who would be willing to participate in this activity by responding to the interview questions. Try to find three individuals who differ demographically (such as age, gender, or ethnicity).

Obtain informed consent. Explain the purpose of the interview and be sure that the interviewee understands that his or her responses may be discussed in class or included in a written report.

Assure and maintain confidentiality. Be sure you tell your interviewee that you will not in any way attach his or her name to the responses in reporting or discussing the responses to the interview. It is critical that you maintain this confidentiality. For many people, nicknames represent very personal experiences.

Conduct the interview. Ask the interview questions in the order in which they appear in this exercise. If the participant seems to be having difficulty with a question, you may read him or her the additional prompts within the brackets following questions 2 through 4.

Summarize the interview data. Respond to the questions in the reaction section of this activity to assess the functions of the nicknames of your interviewees.

Provide feedback to the interviewee if appropriate. If you have some general conclusions about nicknames based on analyzing the interview data you might convey these conclusions to your interviewee. Be sure to thank him or her for the time spent assisting you with this activity.

Participant A

1. By what nickname(s) have you been called?

2. Who called you by this nickname? [For example, family members, peers.]

3. What is the meaning of this nickname? [For example, does it refer to a trait, aspect of your appearance, or a particular incident?]

4. Under what circumstances was this nickname used? [For example, during teasing, expressions of affection, or disciplinary action.]

5. How do you feel about this nickname now?

Participant B

1. By what nickname(s) have you been called?

2. Who called you by this nickname? [For example, family members, peers.]

3. What is the meaning of this nickname? [For example, does it refer to a trait, aspect of your appearance, or a particular incident?]

4. Under what circumstances was this nickname used? [For example, during teasing, expressions of affection, or disciplinary action.]

5. How do you feel about this nickname now?

Participant C

1. By what nickname(s) have you been called?

2. Who called you by this nickname? [For example, family members, peers.]

3. What is the meaning of this nickname? [For example, does it refer to a trait, aspect of your appearance, or a particular incident?]

4. Under what circumstances was this nickname used? [For example, during teasing, expressions of affection, or disciplinary action.]

5. How do you feel about this nickname now?

Reactions: Shoshana Blum-Kulka and Tamar Katriel (1991) derived five functions of nicknames from their study of nickname use in Israeli and Jewish American families. Read the descriptions of the categories below.

The individuating function -- Nicknames that are based on personal characteristics or incidents may distinguish someone from other members of his or her family or community.

The social demarcation function -- Nicknames may be used to indicate social boundaries if they are used exclusively by a particular group. For example, some nicknames are only used within the family and are never used by friends or other nonfamily members.

The social control function -- Sometime nicknames are used to reinforce power differences between individuals. For example, a parent may use a nickname to soften a directive given to a child.

The expressive function -- Nicknames may be used as a term of endearment or to express affection or to indicate that the user is in a particular mood (often a jovial or affectionate mood).

The framing function -- Nicknames may be used to indicate that an interaction has become playful (with the use of affectionate nicknames) or combative (with the use of derogatory nicknames).

1. Which of the functions above were served by the nicknames of each of your interviewees?

2. What would you predict to be the functions most likely served by nicknames in your culture? Please explain.

3. Vivian DeKlerk and Barbara Bosch (1996) found gender differences in nickname use in their study of South African adolescents. They report more males than females had nicknames and that the nicknames of females were more likely to be affectionate and less likely to be critical or humorous than the nicknames of males. How might you explain such findings? If you interviewed a male and a female, do your results correspond to those of DeKlerk and Bosch?

4. James Skipper and colleagues (1990) have noted that assumptions about social class membership can be based on nicknames, particularly the nicknames of males. Do any of the nicknames of your interviewees reflect social class membership? What might distinguish nicknames associated with lower and upper classes?

References:

Blum-Kulka, S. & Katriel, T. (1991). Nicknaming practices in families: A cross-cultural perspective. In S. Ting-Toomey & F. Korzenny (Eds.), *Cross-cultural interpersonal communication* (pp. 58-78). Newbury Park, CA: Sage.

DeKlerk, V., & Bosch, B. (1996). Nicknames as sex-role stereotypes. *Sex Roles, 35*, 9-10.

Glazier, J. (1987). Nicknames and the transformation of an American Jewish Community: Notes on the anthropology of emotion in the urban midwest. *Ethnology, 26*, 73-85.

Nicholls, C. (1995). Warlpiri nicknaming: A personal memoir. *International Journal of the Sociology of Language, 113*, 137-145.

Skipper, J. K., Leslie, P., & Wilson, B. S. (1990). A teaching technique revisited: Family names, nicknames, and social class. *Teaching Sociology, 18*, 209-213.

Name _____   Date _____

Activity 5.5
TABOO TOPICS ACROSS CULTURES

One aspect of self that appears to differ across cultures is the degree to which we are willing to disclose our personal experiences and beliefs. This activity will allow you to assess your own level of self-disclosure (to a male and to a female) and compare it to Goodwin and Lee's (1994) findings with Chinese and English students.

Directions: Think about a close friend of the **same sex**. Then indicate the degree to which you would be willing to discuss the topics or perform the behaviors listed below with that friend.

Once you have answered all of the items using the 7-point scale below, total and average your scores. A series of questions follow.

It is very likely I would discuss the following						It is very unlikely I would discuss the following
1	2	3	4	5	6	7

1. Your political views (if different from friend's)   1 2 3 4 5 6 7

2. Matters of personal hygiene   1 2 3 4 5 6 7

3. Your religious views   1 2 3 4 5 6 7

4. State of the relationship with the friend   1 2 3 4 5 6 7

5. Relationship between your brothers and sisters   1 2 3 4 5 6 7

6. How you feel about home when away from home   1 2 3 4 5 6 7

7. Relationship between your parents   1 2 3 4 5 6 7

8. Feelings about your parent's decisions   1 2 3 4 5 6 7

9. Feelings about time spent with the family   1 2 3 4 5 6 7

10. Friend of the opposite sex you find attractive   1 2 3 4 5 6 7

11. Break-up of a close friendship   1 2 3 4 5 6 7

12. Level of sexual contact with an opposite sex friend   1 2 3 4 5 6 7

13. Feelings about your friend   1 2 3 4 5 6 7

14. Worries about your personal appearance   1 2 3 4 5 6 7

15. Disturbing dream or nightmare   1 2 3 4 5 6 7

16. Feelings of hurt and rejection   1 2 3 4 5 6 7

17. Personal health problems   1 2 3 4 5 6 7

18. Financial worries or problems   1 2 3 4 5 6 7

19. An exceptional achievement   1 2 3 4 5 6 7

20. Aspirations for the future   1 2 3 4 5 6 7

21. Feelings of contentment   1 2 3 4 5 6 7

22. Childhood fears   1 2 3 4 5 6 7

23. Disturbing memories from the past   1 2 3 4 5 6 7

24. Enjoyable childhood experiences   1 2 3 4 5 6 7

25. Dislike of someone your friend is close to   1 2 3 4 5 6 7

26. Friend's relationship with others   1 2 3 4 5 6 7

27. Causes of past disagreements with your friend   1 2 3 4 5 6 7

28. Friend's bad points   1 2 3 4 5 6 7

29. Sexual fantasies   1 2 3 4 5 6 7

30. Your weaknesses/bad points   1 2 3 4 5 6 7

It is very likely
I would do
the following

It is very unlikely
I would do
the following

1   2   3   4   5   6   7

31. Telling your friend you like them   1 2 3 4 5 6 7

32. Sharing items of clothing   1 2 3 4 5 6 7

33. Crying in front of your friend   1 2 3 4 5 6 7

34. Asking a friend a favor   1 2 3 4 5 6 7

35. Hugging your friend   1 2 3 4 5 6 7

Total score (add responses to the 35 items): _____

Average score: _____

Directions: Think about a close friend of the **opposite sex**. Then indicate the degree to which you would be willing to discuss the topics or perform the behaviors listed below with that friend.

Once you have answered all of the items using the 7-point scale below, total and average your scores. A series of questions follow.

It is very likely I would discuss the following						It is very unlikely I would discuss the following
1	2	3	4	5	6	7

1. Your political views (if different from friend's)   1 2 3 4 5 6 7

2. Matters of personal hygiene   1 2 3 4 5 6 7

3. Your religious views   1 2 3 4 5 6 7

4. State of the relationship with the friend   1 2 3 4 5 6 7

5. Relationship between your brothers and sisters   1 2 3 4 5 6 7

6. How you feel about home when away from home   1 2 3 4 5 6 7

7. Relationship between your parents   1 2 3 4 5 6 7

8. Feelings about your parent's decisions   1 2 3 4 5 6 7

9. Feelings about time spent with the family   1 2 3 4 5 6 7

10. Friend of the opposite sex you find attractive   1 2 3 4 5 6 7

11. Break-up of a close friendship   1 2 3 4 5 6 7

12. Level of sexual contact with an opposite sex friend   1 2 3 4 5 6 7

13. Feelings about your friend   1 2 3 4 5 6 7

14. Worries about your personal appearance   1 2 3 4 5 6 7

15. Disturbing dream or nightmare   1 2 3 4 5 6 7

16. Feelings of hurt and rejection   1 2 3 4 5 6 7

17. Personal health problems   1 2 3 4 5 6 7

18. Financial worries or problems   1 2 3 4 5 6 7

19. An exceptional achievement   1 2 3 4 5 6 7

20. Aspirations for the future   1 2 3 4 5 6 7

21. Feelings of contentment   1 2 3 4 5 6 7

22. Childhood fears   1 2 3 4 5 6 7

23. Disturbing memories from the past   1 2 3 4 5 6 7

24. Enjoyable childhood experiences   1 2 3 4 5 6 7

25. Dislike of someone your friend is close to   1 2 3 4 5 6 7

26. Friend's relationship with others   1 2 3 4 5 6 7

27. Causes of past disagreements with your friend   1 2 3 4 5 6 7

28. Friend's bad points   1 2 3 4 5 6 7

29. Sexual fantasies   1 2 3 4 5 6 7

30. Your weaknesses/bad points   1 2 3 4 5 6 7

It is very likely I would do the following						It is very unlikely I would do the following
1	2	3	4	5	6	7

31. Telling your friend you like them   1 2 3 4 5 6 7

32. Sharing items of clothing   1 2 3 4 5 6 7

33. Crying in front of your friend   1 2 3 4 5 6 7

34. Asking a friend a favor   1 2 3 4 5 6 7

35. Hugging your friend   1 2 3 4 5 6 7

Total score (add responses to the 35 items): _____

Average score: _____

Reactions:
1. Goodwin and Lee found that male Chinese participants had average scores of 113 when disclosing to males and 117 when disclosing to females. Female Chinese participants had average scores of 106 when disclosing to males and 92 when disclosing to females. Male British participants had average scores of 102 when disclosing to males and 109 when disclosing to females. Female British participants had average scores of 91 when disclosing to males and 75 when disclosing to females. Describe how your score compares to Goodwin and Lee's findings.

2. Goodwin and Lee's study was based on Gudykunst and Ting-Toomey's (1988) Cultural Variability Model, which predicts that individualists would engage in riskier interpersonal exchanges than collectivists and thus exhibit greater levels of self-disclosure. To what extent is your level of self-disclosure indicated by your cultural background?

3. Research on self-disclosure generally finds greater levels of self-disclosure among females than males. To what extent do you think your gender role socialization (what you have been taught directly and indirectly about appropriate behavior for your gender) has influenced your level of self-disclosure?

4. Goodwin and Lee also examined clusters of items that deal with different types of topics. Items 5, 6, 7, 8, and 9 address family life; items 27, 28, and 30 address friendship faults; and items 33 and 35 deal with demonstrative behavior. Reexamine your responses to these items and note any patterns below.

5. What concerns might you have about research using self-disclosure scales such as the one in this activity?

Source:
  Taboo topics items from Goodwin, R., & Lee, I. Taboo topics among Chinese and English friends. *Journal of Cross-Cultural Psychology, 25*, 325-338. Copyright (c) 1994 by Sage Publications, Inc.. Reprinted with permission.

References:
  Goodwin, R., & Lee, I. (1994). Taboo topics among Chinese and English friends. *Journal of Cross-Cultural Psychology, 25*, 325-338.
  Gudykunst, W., & Ting-Toomey, S. (1988). *Culture and interpersonal communication.* Newbury Park, CA: Sage.

Name _____   Date _____

Activity 5.6
THE COLORS OF EMOTION

Most people readily associate colors with adjectives of emotion (such as anger, envy, fear, and jealousy). By exploring these associations and comparing your findings to those of cross-cultural research, we may better understand the structure of emotions across cultures.

Directions: For each of the four emotions listed, circle the number on the scale below to indicate the degree to which each color reminds you of that particular emotion.

Does not remind me of this color at all					Very much reminds me of this color
1	2	3	4	5	6

ANGER

1. black   1 2 3 4 5 6

2. green   1 2 3 4 5 6

3. red   1 2 3 4 5 6

4. violet   1 2 3 4 5 6

5. blue   1 2 3 4 5 6

6. white   1 2 3 4 5 6

7. pink   1 2 3 4 5 6

8. yellow   1 2 3 4 5 6

9. brown   1 2 3 4 5 6

10. gray   1 2 3 4 5 6

11. orange   1 2 3 4 5 6

12. purple   1 2 3 4 5 6

Does not remind me
of this color at all

					Very much reminds me of this color
1	2	3	4	5	6

ENVY

1. purple   1 2 3 4 5 6

2. white   1 2 3 4 5 6

3. pink   1 2 3 4 5 6

4. black   1 2 3 4 5 6

5. orange   1 2 3 4 5 6

6. red   1 2 3 4 5 6

7. violet   1 2 3 4 5 6

8. yellow   1 2 3 4 5 6

9. blue   1 2 3 4 5 6

10. gray   1 2 3 4 5 6

11. brown   1 2 3 4 5 6

12. green   1 2 3 4 5 6

Does not remind me of this color at all					Very much reminds me of this color
1	2	3	4	5	6

FEAR

1. yellow   1 2 3 4 5 6

2. brown   1 2 3 4 5 6

3. black   1 2 3 4 5 6

4. red   1 2 3 4 5 6

5. violet   1 2 3 4 5 6

6. purple   1 2 3 4 5 6

7. blue   1 2 3 4 5 6

8. white   1 2 3 4 5 6

9. pink   1 2 3 4 5 6

10. green   1 2 3 4 5 6

11. gray   1 2 3 4 5 6

12. orange   1 2 3 4 5 6

Does not remind me of this color at all					Very much reminds me of this color
1	2	3	4	5	6

JEALOUSY

1. red   1 2 3 4 5 6

2. green   1 2 3 4 5 6

3. gray   1 2 3 4 5 6

4. blue   1 2 3 4 5 6

5. orange   1 2 3 4 5 6

6. white   1 2 3 4 5 6

7. black   1 2 3 4 5 6

8. purple   1 2 3 4 5 6

9. pink   1 2 3 4 5 6

10. brown   1 2 3 4 5 6

11. violet   1 2 3 4 5 6

12. yellow   1 2 3 4 5 6

Scoring: Under each of the four emotions below, list any colors that received a rating of 4 or greater.

Anger   **Envy**   **Fear**   **Jealousy**

Reactions: Please respond to the questions below in the space provided.

1. Summarize your findings:

2. Hupka and colleagues (1997) studied the association between color and emotion in Germany, Mexico, Poland, Russia, and the United States. They found that in all five countries, black and red were associated with anger, black was associated with fear, and red was associated with jealousy. However, there were several cross-cultural differences. Poles also associated purple with anger, envy and jealousy; Germans connected yellow with envy and jealousy; Americans associated black, green, and red with envy; and Russians connected black, purple, and yellow with envy.

Compare your data to the cross-cultural findings described above.

3. What are some metaphors or expressions in your language that associate colors with emotions? Do these correspond to your findings?

4. Some previous studies of color and emotion used actual color chips rather than color words. What methodological problem might arise from the earlier technique? (*Hint*: Check an Introductory Psychology text for the distinction between hue, saturation, and brightness.)

5. Hupka and colleagues predicted and found greater cross-cultural agreement in the colors associated with anger and fear than with envy and jealousy. Based on what you have learned in your classes about the classification of emotions, why would this finding make sense? (*Hint*: Check an Introductory Psychology text for models classifying emotions.)

Source:
    Rating scale adapted from Hupka, R. B., Zalenski, Z., Otto, J., Reidl, L., & Tarabrina, N. V. The colors of anger, envy, fear, and jealousy: A cross-cultural study. *Journal of Cross-Cultural Psychology, 28*, 156-171. Copyright (c) 1997 by Sage Publications, Inc. Adapted with permission.

Reference:
    Hupka, R. B., Zalenski, Z., Otto, J., Reidl, L., & Tarabrina, N. V. (1997). The colors of anger, envy, fear, and jealousy: A cross-cultural study. *Journal of Cross-Cultural Psychology, 28*, 156-171.

Name _____   Date _____

Activity 5.7
CULTURAL DISPLAY RULES

Studies by Paul Ekman and Wallace Friesen (Ekman, 1972) and others have indicated that several emotions tend to be universal in that they can be recognized across cultures. However, as most sojourners have learned, there is great variability in the *expression* of emotions across cultures. Ekman and Friesen attribute this to the presence of *cultural display rules* that dictate the appropriate expression of emotions for a particular setting. This activity is designed to familiarize you with the concept of cultural display rules and to help you to identify the display rules you follow.

Directions: Over the next day or two, keep a record of your emotions and their expression. When you experience an identifiable emotion, make an entry below indicating when you experienced the emotion; the type of emotion you experienced (such as happiness, sadness, fear, anger, disgust or surprise); the setting in which you experienced the emotion (Were you alone or with others? Were you in a public or private place?); and the manner in which the emotion was expressed (Indicate the form -- such as laughing, yelling, or frowning -- and the intensity of the expression). Try to record 10 instances of emotional expression.

	Date/Time	Emotion	Setting	Expression (form/intensity)
1				
2				
3				
4				
5				

6				
7				
8				
9				
10				

Reactions:

1. Compare the instances of emotional expression that took place in private rather than public settings. What do you conclude about the display rules governing the public expression of emotion?

2. Compare the instances of emotional expression involving different types of emotions. Did you observe different rules governing the expression of positive (happiness, surprise) as opposed to negative (sadness, anger) emotions?

3. To what extent can you trace your display rules to your cultural background or gender socialization. Please explain.

4. How do you think cultural display rules might affect intercultural communication?

Reference:
    Ekman, P. (1972). Universal and cultural differences in facial expression of emotion. In J. R. Cole (Ed.), *Nebraska symposium on motivation, 1971* (pp. 207-283). Lincoln: University of Nebraska Press.

Name _____   Date _____

Activity 5.8
THE CULTURE AND PERSONALITY SCHOOL

In the 1930s and 1940s, a major research focus of psychological anthropologists was the study of culture and personality. These studies were strongly influenced by Freudian research and often involved the use of psychoanalytic assessment tools (such as the Rorschach ink blots) to identify the basic personality type characterizing members of a specific culture. For example, in 1944 Cora DuBois published an analysis of the Alorese based on her extensive fieldwork in a small mountain village in the Dutch East Indies. In this book she discussed the connection between childrearing practices and adult character. Her data included ethnographic descriptions as well as the results of several psychological tests. She concluded that the structure of day-to-day activities led to the neglect of Alorese children and that this level of neglect resulted in such personality characteristics as emotional instability and distrust. DuBois' study typifies the culture and personality school. The purpose of this activity is to examine the assumptions underlying this significant area of research on culture and human behavior.

Directions: Read, and then evaluate, each of the five assumptions of the Culture and Personality School stated below (adapted from Bock, 1995).

1. *The continuity assumption* -- Early childhood experiences (such as weaning and toilet training) are the primary determinants of adult personality. Similar childhood experiences are assumed to result in similar adult personality configurations.

2. *The uniformity assumption* -- Societies can be described in terms of a core personality type. A corollary of this assumption is that childrearing behaviors are culturally patterned and are thus fairly similar for families within a culture.

3. *The causal assumption* -- Basic personality structure is an entity that is not only observable but can cause, or be caused by, cultural institutions. For example, if a society is characterized as having a core personality trait of aggression, that trait can be described as causing a practice such as intergroup warfare. Yet the evidence for the core trait of aggression may come from observing such practices as intergroup warfare.

4. *The projective assumption* -- By using projective tests (such as Rorschach ink blots) it is possible to determine basic personality characteristics and unconscious conflicts. Further, it is assumed that projective tests can be effectively used to understand the psychological makeup of an individual who is a member of a markedly different culture from the one in which the test was developed and standardized.

5. *The objectivity assumption* -- Cultural outsiders are able to accurately describe psychological characteristics and culturally pattern behaviors without imposing culture-bound values or interpretations.

Source:
   The five assumptions of the Culture and Personality School were adapted from Bock, P. K. *Rethinking psychological anthropology: Continuity and change in the study of human action.* Copyright (c) 1995 by Waveland Press. Adapted with permission.

Reference:
   DuBois, C. (1944). *The people of Alor.* New York: Harper & Row.

Name _____   Date _____

Activity 5.9
DEAR SIGMUND (OR CARL)

The major personality theorists in psychology come from a similar European or Euro-American tradition in terms of the cultural values and assumptions inherent in the theories. This activity encourages you to think about personality theory from a cross-cultural perspective.

Directions: Select the personality theory of either Sigmund Freud or Carl Rogers. Below, make some notes about important concepts in the theory you chose. Then write a one-page letter in the space provided (on the next page) to one of these theorists that identifies aspects of the theory that are culture bound and makes recommendations for revision. Remember that ideas about gender are a part of our cultural values. Some suggestions are provided for concepts you might include in your consideration of each theory. It may also be helpful to refer to an introductory psychology or personality theories textbook for an overview of the theory you chose.

Freudian Theory -- some concepts for cultural consideration: psychosexual stages; superego development; psychoanalysis; the use of projective tests.

Rogerian Theory -- some concepts for cultural consideration: the self; unconditional positive regard; the fully functioning person; client-centered therapy.

Notes:

Dear_____,

Name _____   Date _____

Activity 5.10
CULTURE AND THE BIG FIVE

A major area of research in personality psychology has focused on identifying underlying dimensions of personality. Studies conducted by different researchers using a variety of measures have found support for the existence of five basic personality traits (see, for example, McCrae & Costa, 1987; Digman, 1990). These dimensions are often referred to as the *Big Five*. There is considerable cross-cultural evidence for the generality of the Big Five traits (see, for example, Paunonen et al., 1996; Stumpf, 1993). However, the measures used to assess personality in these studies were developed primarily by researchers with a "Western" orientation to psychology. More recent research has used an emic approach to personality assessment to explore the possibility of indigenous dimensions of personality (see, for example, Cheung and colleagues, 1996).   This activity will explore the cross-cultural applicability of the Big Five.

Directions: There are three steps to this activity. First, in the column on the left side of the page, list 10 traits that describe you or someone you know. Second, read the descriptions of the Big Five traits on the next page and indicate in the column on the right the Big Five trait category under which each of the traits on the left would fall. If the trait on the left does not fit clearly into any of the Big Five categories, then leave the corresponding Big Five space blank. Finally, read about three indigenous personality traits and determine whether these fit under the Big Five classifications.

Trait	Big Five Category
1. _____	_____
2. _____	_____
3. _____	_____
4. _____	_____
5. _____	_____
6. _____	_____
7. _____	_____
8. _____	_____
9. _____	_____
10. _____	_____

The Big Five (adapted from McCrae & Costa, 1997):

Openness -- Refers to the degree to which one is imaginative versus down-to-earth, prefers variety versus routine, and is independent versus conforming.

Conscientiousness -- Refers to the degree to which one is organized versus disorganized, careful versus careless, and self-disciplined versus weak willed.

Extraversion -- Refers to the degree to which one is sociable versus introverted, fun loving versus sober, and affectionate versus reserved.

Agreeableness -- Refers to the degree to which one is softhearted versus ruthless, trusting versus suspicious, and helpful versus uncooperative.

Neuroticism -- Refers to the degree to which one is worried versus calm, insecure versus secure, and self-pitying versus self-satisfied.

1. Listed below are three traits considered to be indigenous aspects of personality. Read the descriptions of these traits and determine which Big Five category, if any, could be used to classify the trait.

Trait and Definition   **Big Five Category**

- *Philotimo* (see discussion in Triandis
  & Vassiliou, 1972) involves being polite,
  generous, respectful, and meeting one's
  obligations. [Greek]   _____

- *Filial piety* (see Zhang & Bond, 1998)
  involves obeying and respecting
  parents, ancestors, and those in
  positions senior to oneself. Children
  should provide for the mental and
  physical well-being of parents and
  behave in a way that brings honor
  upon one's family name. [Chinese]   _____

- *Amae* (see Doi, 1973) refers to a
  combination of childlike dependence
  on and obligation to another person.
  Rooted in the mother-child relationship,
  amae is also seen as characterizing the
  relationship between people of higher
  and lower status. [Japanese]   _____

2. Based on your findings, what do you conclude about the universality of the Big Five?

3. Discuss below how you would design a more thorough and valid test of the universality of the Big Five.

Source:

The Big Five descriptions were adapted from McCrae, R. R. & Costa, P. T. (1987). Validation of the five factor model of personality across instruments and observers. *Journal of Personality and Social Psychology, 52,* 81-90.

References:

Cheung, F. M., Leung, K., Fan, R. M., Song, W.-Z., Zhang, J.-X., & Zhang, J.-P. (1996). Development of the Chinese personality assessment inventory. *Journal of Cross-Cultural Psychology, 27,* 181-199.

Digman, J. M. (1990). Personality structure: Emergence of the five-factor model. *Annual Review of Psychology, 41,* 417-440.

Doi, T. (1973). *The anatomy of dependence.* New York: Harper Row.

McCrae, R. R. & Costa, P. T. (1987). Validation of the five factor model of personality across instruments and observers. *Journal of Personality and Social Psychology, 52,* 81-90.

Paunonen, S. V., Keinonen, M., Trzebinski, J., Forsterling, F., Grishenko-Roze, N., Kouznetsova, L, & Chan, D. W. (1996). The structure of personality in six cultures. *Journal of Cross-Cultural Psychology, 27,* 339-353.

Stumpf, H. (1993). The factor structure of the Personality Research Form: A cross-national evaluation. *Journal of Personality, 61,* 27-48.

Triandis, H. C., & Vassiliou, V. (1972). Comparative analysis of subjective culture. In H. C. Triandis (Ed.), *The analysis of subjective culture* (pp. 299-338). New York: Wiley.

Zhang, J., & Bond, M. H. (1998). Personality and filial piety among college students in two Chinese societies: The added value of indigenous constructs. *Journal of Cross-Cultural Psychology, 29,* 402-417.

Chapter 6. Health, Stress, and Coping Across Cultures

Name _____   Date _____

Activity 6.1
WHAT IS ABNORMAL?

Before exploring issues of culture and well-being, it is useful to consider what we mean when we talk about behavior that is normal or abnormal. This activity focuses on exploring these concepts.

Directions: Please respond to each of the questions below.

1. Describe a behavior that, within your culture, is/was considered abnormal at one point in history, but normal at another point in history.

2. Describe a behavior that, within your culture, is considered abnormal in one setting, but is considered normal in another setting.

3. Describe a behavior that is considered normal in your culture, but abnormal in some other culture(s).

4. Describe a behavior that is considered abnormal in your culture, but normal in some other culture(s).

5. Describe a behavior that is considered abnormal in all societies.

6. Develop a set of criteria that can be used to determine if a behavior is abnormal.

7. Would the criteria you developed likely apply across cultures? Please explain.

Name _____   Date _____

Activity 6.2
CULTURE AND HEALTH: THE NI HON SAN STUDY

Several studies of culture and health have taken advantage of what one might consider a natural experiment; that is, changes in health as a specific ethnic group migrates to another culture. By comparing the health measures of members of an ethnic group who do not migrate with those who do, it is possible to separate genetic from behavioral influences on health. An example of this type of research is the Ni Hon San study described below. The purpose of this activity is to encourage you to think about how culturally imbedded behaviors may influence health. In addition, this activity will familiarize you with a form of research that provides significant insights into issues of culture and health.

Directions: Read the description of the Ni Hon San study below (based on Benfante, 1992) and then answer the questions that follow.

The Ni Hon San Study

The Ni Hon San study began in 1964 as part of the ongoing Honolulu Heart Study. This research compared health data from three groups of men: Japanese men living in Hiroshima and Nagasaki, Japan; descendants of Japanese migrants to Hawaii; and descendants of Japanese migrants to San Francisco, California. One of the most striking findings of this study is that the rate of cardiovascular disease (heart disease) was lowest in the Japan group, highest in the California group, and intermediate in the Hawaii group.

1. What conclusions can you draw from the findings of the Ni Hon San study about the role of genetics and behavior in the development of cardiovascular disease?

2. What assumptions can you make about the distinction between individuals of Japanese ancestry living in Hawaii as opposed to California?

3. List some behavioral factors (things people do in daily life) that may have affected the findings of the Ni Hon San study.

4. List some environmental factors (aspects of the setting in which people live) that may have affected the findings of the Ni Hon San study.

5. The participants of the Ni Hon San study were all male. Would you have any concerns about extrapolating from this study to draw conclusions about the health practices of women? Please explain.

6. Think about another ethnic group with which you are familiar that has migrated from one culture to another. Identify this group.

7. What behavioral changes might accompany migration for the group you described above.

8. How might these behavioral changes affect health?

Reference:
    Benfante, R. (1992). Studies of cardiovascular disease and cause-specific mortality trends in Japanese-American men living in Hawaii and risk factor comparisons with other Japanese populations in the Pacific region: A review. *Human Biology, 64*, 791-805.

Name _____   Date _____

Activity 6.3
CULTURE AND THE TREATMENT
AND PREVENTION OF AIDS

Health professionals involved in the treatment and prevention of acquired immune deficiency syndrome (AIDS) have recently begun to address the cultural factors involved in their work. Culture is relevant to AIDS in that it influences beliefs about illness and sexual practices, language use and communication style, family roles and structure, and religious beliefs. The purpose of this activity is to familiarize you with some of the cultural considerations in the prevention and treatment of AIDS.

Directions: Read the three descriptions below. Following each, explain how you might address the treatment or prevention of AIDS in a manner appropriate to the cultural context.

1. Pamela Balls Organista and Kurt C. Organista (1998) have identified Mexican migrant workers in the United States (primarily laborers and seasonal farmworkers) as a new at-risk population for AIDS. These authors point to such risk factors as prostitution use, male homosexual contact, limited knowledge regarding HIV transmission and proper condom use, and female migrants having high-risk sexual partners. Balls Organista and Organista explain that programs for treating and preventing AIDS face cultural barriers in that:

- Mexican migrant workers may have limited literacy and English speaking ability.

- There is a tendency for traditional Latino men and women to avoid directly discussing sexual matters.

- Migrant workers are by definition a transient group.

- Migrant workers often live in conditions of poverty.

- Mexican migrant women tend to believe that carrying condoms makes one promiscuous.

Discuss below how you might address AIDS prevention with this population.

2. Stan Sesser (1994) explains that there is such stigma attached to AIDS in Japan that the Japanese Ministry of Health and Welfare has funded an HIV testing clinic in Hawaii for Japanese citizens. AIDS is viewed particularly negatively since, from a Japanese perspective, it is associated with homosexuality and with foreigners. According to Sesser, those who fly to Hawaii to be tested often state that the plane fare for the 4,000 mile trip is well worth the guarantee of anonymity because public knowledge of being HIV positive would be disastrous in Japan. Describe below how you might address HIV testing in Japan.

3. A relatively new class of drugs, called *protease inhibitors*, has greatly decreased deaths from AIDS where the drugs are available. African Americans as a group, however, have not benefitted from the availability of these drugs to the extent expected by health professionals. Some health professionals and AIDS patients have attributed this in part to the fact that protease inhibitors are experimental and may trigger memories of the Tuskegee study of the 1930s in which researchers studied the effects of syphilis by allowing hundreds of infected African American men to go untreated (Wilson, 1997). Describe how you might address AIDS treatment with this population.

References:

Balls Organista, P., & Organista, K. C. (1998). Culture and gender sensitive AIDS prevention with Mexican migrant laborers: A primer for counselors. In P. Balls Organista, K. M. Chun, & G. Marin (Eds.), *Readings in ethnic psychology* (pp. 240-246). New York: Routledge.

Wilson, B. (Reporter). (1997, May 16). Tuskeegee Study's legacy of mistrust. *All things considered*. Washington, DC: National Public Radio.

Sesser, S. (1994, November 14). Hidden death: A letter from Japan. *New Yorker*. Excerpted in Living Well Project: Asian and Pacific Islander AIDS Services (1995). *Sexual diversity handbook*. San Francisco, CA: Author.

Name _____ Date _____

Activity 6.4
EXPLAINING CULTURAL DIFFERENCES IN DRINKING BEHAVIOR

Cross-cultural research on alcohol use and abuse has uncovered a wide range of drinking behaviors and attitudes. The purpose of this activity is to think about the connection between culture and drinking behavior.

Directions: For each of the research findings stated below, create a hypothesis to explain why these findings may have occurred. You will need to think about the role of culture in each of the findings. Remember that culture may be *confounded* with such variables as social class, ethnicity, physiological differences, and legislation.

1. **Research Finding:** A large number of studies indicate that people of Asian ancestry tend to be at a lower risk for developing alcohol-related disorders than people of European or African ancestry (Whitfield, 1997). How might culture impact the development of alcohol-related diseases?

Hypothesis:

2. **Research Finding:** Oye Gureje, J. L. Vazqueze-Barquero, and Aleksandar Janca (1996) studied the concept of normal drinking in nine different countries (Canada, Greece, India, Korea, Mexico, Romania, Switzerland, Turkey, and the United States-- including the Navajo Nation in the United States). Their research found a wide range of quantities associated with normal drinking. In some cultures (India and Navajo) most people did not accept the concept of "normal drinking." How might culture relate to perceptions of normal drinking behavior?

Hypothesis:

3. **Research Finding:** Harold Rosenberg, Eric Devine, and Nan Rothrock (1996) surveyed 335 Canadian alcohol treatment centers regarding the acceptability of moderate drinking (as opposed to abstinence) as a treatment goal. They found that Canadian agencies were more accepting of moderate drinking for alcoholics than American agencies, but less accepting than British or Norwegian agencies. How might culture impact the acceptability of moderate drinking as a treatment goal?

Hypothesis:

References:

Gureje, O., Vazquez-Barquero, J. L., & Janca, A. (1996). Comparisons of alcohol and other drugs: Experience from the WHO collaborative cross-cultural applicability research (CAR) study. *Addiction, 91,* 1529-1538.

Rosenberg, H., Devine, E. G., Rothrock, N. (1996). Acceptance of moderate drinking by alcoholism treatment services in Canada. *Journal of Studies on Alcohol, 57,* 559-562.

Whitfield, J. B. (1997). Meta-analysis of the effects of alcohol dehydrogenase genotype on alcohol dependence and alcoholic liver disease. *Alcohol and Alcoholism, 32,* 613-619.

Name _____   Date _____

Activity 6.5
CULTURE AND MENTAL HEALTH SELF QUIZ

In recent decades, a large number of books and articles have been published on issues of culture and mental health. This activity will enable you to test your knowledge of a variety of findings from this literature.

Directions: Decide whether each of the statements below is true or false. Then check your answers on page 379.

1. Depression and schizophrenia appear to be universal in that these mental illnesses have been found across cultures studied.   TRUE / FALSE

2. The likelihood of recovering from schizophrenia is greater for patients in nonindustrialized societies than industrialized societies.   TRUE / FALSE

3. Cross-cultural research has consistently found a ratio of about two women diagnosed with depression for every one man with with the disorder.   TRUE / FALSE

4. A syndrome widely discussed in Japan is a form of work-related stress that translates as "death by overwork."   TRUE / FALSE

5. Anorexia nervosa, a syndrome marked by self-starvation and a distorted body image, is specific to the relatively affluent cultures of North America and Europe.   TRUE / FALSE

6. Chinese psychiatrists are more likely to hospitalize a patient with symptoms of depression than with symptoms of mania.   TRUE / FALSE

7. African American, Asian American, and Mexican American clients are judged to have higher levels of mental health functioning if they are diagnosed by ethnically matched therapists than if they are diagnosed by ethnically different therapists.   TRUE / FALSE

8. People in most cultures express feelings of depression as some form of feeling "down."   TRUE / FALSE

9. People in individualist countries report more stress-related illnesses than do people in collectivist countries.   TRUE / FALSE

10. Across cultures, seeking social support is the preferred style
of coping with stress.   TRUE / FALSE

Name _____   Date _____

Activity 6.6
ALTERED STATES OF CONSCIOUSNESS

The term *altered states of consciousness (ASC)* is typically used to refer to conditions other than the waking state of awareness. ASC include sleep, daydreams, meditative or trance states, and states induced by drugs or alcohol. Anthropological research indicates that ASC are very common across cultures. In fact, in one study of 488 societies, 90% exhibited forms of possession or trance states (Bourguignon & Evascu, 1977). The purpose of this activity is to explore how the cultural context in which these ASC occur impacts the perception and experience of these states.

Directions: Read and respond to the questions below.

1. Read the discussion of ASC in a recent introductory psychology textbook. What type of ASC have been induced by psychologists in a laboratory setting? In what nonlaboratory settings do ASC also take place?

2. In the United States, the American Indian Religious Freedom Act, passed in 1994, permits members of the Native American Church to use peyote in religious ceremonies. Peyote, the "buttons" of a small cactus with hallucinogenic properties, is not legal for use by other Americans. More recently, a draft rule was proposed by the U. S. Pentagon which would allow the use of peyote by Native American U. S. soldiers for religious purposes. In the past, American Indian soldiers have reported being threatened, excluded from high-risk jobs, and discouraged from acknowledging their membership in the Native American Church. According to the guidelines of this ruling, peyote may not be used or possessed aboard military vehicles or on military installations (Mendoza, 1997). Do you agree with this ruling? Please explain.

3. Wallace (1959) found distinct differences between Anglo-Americans and Native Americans in response to mescaline (a peyote derivative) intoxication. Whereas the Anglo-Americans demonstrated extreme mood shifts, a removal of inhibitions (manifested in inappropriate sexual and aggressive behavior), and feelings of meaningless, the Native Americans demonstrated relatively stable moods, no inappropriate behavior, and an increased sense of personal worth. What explanation can you give for these findings regarding the way this particular ASC is experienced?

4. Colleen Ward (1989) states that in most cultures ASC are not viewed as forms of pathology or abnormal behavior. In fact, she suggests that ASC serve an adaptive function. How might certain ASC be adaptive, that is, beneficial to survival in some cultures?

References:

Bourguignon, E., & Evascu, T. (1977). Altered states of consciousness within a general evolutionary perspective: A holocultural analysis. *Behavior Science Research, 12,* 199-216.

Mendoza, M. (April 16, 1997). Military will allow religious peyote use. *The Seattle Times.*

Wallace, A. F. C. (1959). Cultural determinants of response to hallucinatory experience. *American Anthropologist, 1,* 58-69.

Ward, C. (Ed.). (1989). *Altered states of consciousness and mental health.* Newbury Park, CA: Sage

Name _____   Date _____

Activity 6.7
CULTURE-SPECIFIC DISORDERS

One fascinating area of research on culture and mental health focuses on *culture-specific disorders* (also known as *culture-bound syndromes*). These terms refer to forms of mental illness that are unique to a certain culture or locale. Researchers have taken two major approaches to understanding culture-specific disorders. One approach, the *universalist* view, holds that there exist similarities in mental disorders across cultures, but the expression of these disorders differs from culture to culture. Universalistic researchers might focus on evidence that depression and schizophrenia can be identified in cultures throughout the world (see, for example, World Health Organization, 1979; 1983). A second perspective, the *cultural relativist* approach, suggests that some disorders are unique to a specific culture and may only be understood within the context of that culture (see, for example, Kirmayer, 1991). Relativistic researchers focus on the distinctive cultural features of some mental disorders. This activity was designed to encourage you to explore these two perspectives on culture and mental illness.

Directions: Choose a culture-specific disorder to investigate using your library resources (such as books on culture and psychopathology or journal articles indexed in PsycLIT or PsycINFO). Several culture-specific disorders are listed below, though you may discover others in your search. Before you start, read through the questions that follow and be prepared to address these with the information you gather.

amok	brain fag	latah
ataque de nervios	dhat	pibloktoq
bilis and colera	hwa-byung	susto
boufee dilerante	koro	zar

1. Identify and describe the disorder you selected (Where does it take place? Who is affected by it? What is perceived to be the cause? What are the accompanying symptoms?).

2. One way to combine the two perspectives on culture-specific disorders is to identify both the etic (universal) and emic (culture-specific) aspects of the disorder (Beardsley, 1994; Beardsley & Pedersen, 1997). For example, Lisa Marie Beardsley (1994) has used this approach (below) to depict the symptoms of *taijin-kyofusho*, a type of social phobia found in Japan. In this disorder patients, primarily males, become fearful that they will offend others by such acts as staring, blushing, or emitting odors.

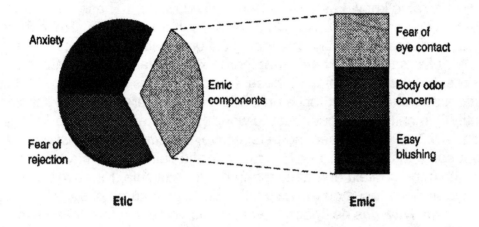

Etic and emic aspects of social phobias (as illustrated by Taijin-Kyofusho)

Source: Beardsley (1994).

In the space provided below, diagram the emic and the etic components of the syndrome you investigated. An introductory psychology or abnormal psychology textbook may be a helpful resource for identifying the etic components.

3. Tanaka Matsumi and Draguns (1997) caution that universal systems for classifying disorders may lose sight of important aspects of the cultural context. For example, Draguns (1973) observed that the expression of mental disorders within a specified culture tends to be an *exaggeration of the normal*. In the case of taijin-kyofusho, the symptoms expressed indicate an exaggeration of the Japanese value of sensitivity toward others (Tanaka-Matsumi & Draguns, 1997). Consider the cultural context of the disorder you investigated. Can this disorder be viewed as an exaggeration of the normal? Please explain.

4. Do you endorse a universalist or a cultural relativist approach to classifying mental disorders? Please explain.

Source:
    Figure reprinted from Beardsley, L. M. Medical diagnosis and treatment across cultures. In W. J. Lonner, & R. S. Malpass (Eds.), *Psychology and culture* (pp. 279-284). Copyright (c) 1994 by Allyn & Bacon. Reprinted with permission.

References:
    Beardsley, L. M. (1994). Medical diagnosis and treatment across cultures. In W. J. Lonner, & R. S. Malpass (Eds.), *Psychology and culture* (pp. 279-284). Boston: Allyn & Bacon.
    Beardsley, L. M., & Pedersen, P. (1997). Health and culture-centered intervention. In J. W. Berry, M. H. Segall, & C. Kagitcibasi (Eds). *Handbook of cross-cultural psychology: Vol. 3* (2nd ed., pp. 413-448). Boston: Allyn & Bacon.
    Draguns, J. (1973). Comparison of psychopathology across cultures: Issues, findings, directions. *Journal of Cross-Cultural Psychology, 4*, 9-47.
    Kirmayer, L. J. (1991). The place of culture in psychiatric nosology: Taijin Kyofusho and DSM III-R. *Journal of Nervous and Mental Disorder, 179*, 19-28.
    Tanaka-Matsumi, J., & Draguns, J. (1997). Culture and psychopathology. In J. W. Berry, M. H. Segall, & C. Kagitcibasi (Eds). *Handbook of cross-cultural psychology: Vol. 3* (2nd ed., pp. 449-491). Boston: Allyn & Bacon.
    World Health Organization. (1979). *Schizophrenia: An international follow-up study.* New York: Wiley.
    World Health Organization. (1983). *Depressive disorders in different cultures: Report of the WHO collaborative study of standardized assessment of depressive disorders.* Geneva: World Health Organization.

Name _____   Date _____

Activity 6.8
SELF-HELP AND WELL-BEING

This activity explores how well-being is viewed in the dominant culture by examining books that provide advice on how to improve one's life (self-help books).

Directions: For this activity you will need to make a visit to your local bookstore or public library and investigate the self-help section (sometimes self-help books are categorized under Psychology). Spend some time looking at a good sampling of self-help books and then answer the questions below.

1. Based on the self-help books you examined, list three to five titles of books addressing the well-being of women. (You will need to decide if the intended audience is women.)

2. Based on the self-help books you examined, list three to five titles of books addressing the well-being of men. (You will need to decide if the intended audience is men.)

3. List the titles of any self-help books that support individualist goals (such as independence, assertiveness, or individual achievement).

4. List the titles of any self-help books that support collectivist goals (such as family harmony, fitting in to the group, or working as a team).

5. You may find that self-help books tend to address the well-being of some groups and ignore others. List some topics that you would add to make the collection of self-help groups more inclusive of diversity.

6. Based on your examination of self-help books, how might the dominant culture define well-being?

7. Consider for a moment the concept of self-help book. What cultural values underlie this phenomenon?

Name _____ Date _____

Activity 6.9
CLIENT'S AND COUNSELOR'S THOUGHTS

Research on multicultural counseling indicates that when clients and counselors come from different cultural backgrounds there is a greater likelihood that the client will terminate the therapy sooner and have less satisfactory outcomes (Atkinson & Lowe, 1995). Pamela Hays (1996) suggests that it is important for counselors to examine their own biases and inexperience regarding cultural and social groups. Her *ADRESSING* model focuses on the interacting cultural influences of age, disability, race, ethnicity, social status, sexual orientation, indigenous heritage, national origin, and gender. Some approaches to training practitioners of multicultural counseling, such as Paul Pedersen's (1994) Triad Model, use complex role plays in which participants other than those enacting the client and counselor make the cultural issues explicit. This activity, based on these approaches, encourages you to consider some of the complexities of multicultural counseling and the preparation of counselor trainees for intercultural interaction.

Directions: For this activity you are asked to write two versions of a scenario that illustrates cultural differences between a client and counselor. The first version should consist of a dialogue between a client and a counselor in which there is some cultural misunderstanding or misperception that is NOT verbalized. In the second version, make the cultural issues explicit by including the thoughts of the client and of the counselor (see the example below). Be sure that you use this activity as an opportunity to dispel -- rather than create -- stereotypes. It is also important to remember that there is a great deal of variability within any social group, and the cultural differences illustrated in this activity should be thought of as illustrating dimensions on which *cultures* may differ, but not a guide for determining the behavior or attitudes of particular *individuals*. The example below addresses age as a factor in a client-counselor interaction.

Example:
The following is a counseling session involving a 32-year-old male psychotherapist, Dr. Allen, and a 70-year-old female client, Mrs. Green.

Counselor. Come right in, Mrs. Green, I hope I haven't kept you waiting long.

Client: That's quite alright, I brought something to do in the waiting room.

Counselor. Well, fine. Now tell me why you've come to see me today.

Client: Well, I've been having some trouble with my mind.

Counselor: What do you mean, Mrs. Green?

Client: I guess it might be called "writer's block," but it's been going on for some time now and I'm rather concerned about it.

Counselor: Now when did you first realize you were having trouble with your memory?

Client: Uh. . .um . . . it's not my memory exactly . . . um it's more like my ability to generate creative new ideas in my writing. You see, after I retired from teaching I took up writing novels and uh . . .

Counselor: Mrs. Green, maybe you need some other activities. There's a crafts class right here at the clinic on Thursdays.

Client: Well, maybe I'll check into it.

Counselor: In the meantime, let's make an appointment for the same time next week.

Client: That should be fine, Dr. Allen. See you then.

The second version of the scenario includes the thoughts of the client and counselor:

The following is a counseling session involving a 32-year-old male psychotherapist, Dr. Allen, and a 70-year-old female client, Mrs. Green.

Counselor: Come right in, Mrs. Green, I hope I haven't kept you waiting long.

[*Counselor's Thoughts*: I hope I haven't made her cranky or anything.]

Client: That's quite alright, I brought something to do in the waiting room.

[*Counselor's Thoughts*: Oh, that bag must be full of knitting or needlepoint.]

[*Client's Thoughts*: Good thing I brought my manuscript to work on. I had no idea I'd have to wait for such a long time.]

Counselor: Well, fine. Now tell me why you've come to see me today.

[*Counselor's Thoughts*: I guess this isn't going to be one of my most exciting mornings.]

Client: Well, I've been having some trouble with my mind.

Counselor: What do you mean, Mrs. Green?

[*Counselor's Thoughts*: Oh gosh, probably Alzheimer's!]

Client: I guess it might be called "writer's block," but it's been going on for some time now and I'm rather concerned about it.

Counselor: Now when did you first realize you were having trouble with your memory?

[*Counselor's Thoughts*: Talk about memory problems...I can't seem to recall what I learned in graduate school about the diagnostic criteria for senile dementia.]

Client: Uh...um...it's not my memory exactly...um it's more like my ability to generate creative new ideas in my writing.

[*Client's Thoughts*: I get it! He thinks I'm senile!]

Client: You see, after I retired from teaching I took up writing novels and uh. . .

[*Client's Thoughts*: He's looking at me like I'm crazy. This is so unnerving.]

[*Counselor's Thoughts*: Hmm. . . she forgot the end of her sentence. Not a good sign in terms of cognitive abilities.]

Counselor: Mrs. Green, maybe you need some other activities. . . there's a crafts class right here at the clinic on Thursdays.

[*Counselor's Thoughts*: She just needs to stay busy.]

Client: Well, maybe I'll check into it.

[*Client's Thoughts*: He doesn't understand my situation at all. I guess it was a big mistake to go to a counselor.]

Counselor: In the meantime, let's make an appointment for the same time next week.

[*Counselor's Thoughts*: I guess I should get her back to make a more thorough diagnosis of her memory deficits.]

Client: That should be fine, Dr. Allen. See you then.

[*Client's Thoughts*: I'll call and cancel the appointment as soon as I get home.]

Write your dialogue (without client or counselor thoughts) in the space below:

Write your dialogue (with client and counselor thoughts) in the space below:

References:

Atkinson, D. R., & Lowe, S. M. (1995). The role of ethnicity, cultural knowledge, and conventional techniques in counseling and psychotherapy. In J. G. Ponterotto, J. M. Casas, L. A. Suzuki, & C. M. Alexander (Eds.), *Handbook of multicultural counseling* (pp. 387-414). Thousand Oaks, CA: Sage.

Hays, P. A. (1996). Addressing the complexities of culture and gender in counseling. *Journal of Counseling and Development, 74,* 332-338.

Pedersen, P. (1994). Simulating the client's internal dialogue as a counselor training technique. *Simulation and Gaming, 25,* 40-50.

Name _____   Date _____

Activity 6.10
CULTURE AND PSYCHOTHERAPY

This exercise will explore the ways in which your conception of therapy may be culture bound and will help you to better understand one *indigenous* form of psychotherapy.

Directions: Use the space provided to respond to the questions below.

1. You are probably familiar with the use of psychotherapy to treat emotional or psychological difficulties. You may have read about therapy, seen therapists in the media, may know someone who has been to a therapist, or may have been to a therapist yourself. Based on your image of therapy, please define the term "therapy" below.

2. List some of the major features of therapy.

In the 1920s, a Japanese psychiatrist name Shoma Morita developed a therapy to treat neuroses that is based in part on Buddhist principles. It focuses on rest and isolation (in fact, Reynolds, 1976, observed a sign in one Morita clinic that read "People who converse will not get well"). The therapy generally lasts from 4 to 8 weeks and consists of the following stages (as outlined by Prince, 1980, p.299):

a. Total bed rest and isolation for 4 to 10 days; the patient
   is totally inactive and not permitted to converse, read, write,
   or listen to the radio.

b. For the next 7 to 14 days, the patient is out of bed and allowed
   to do light work in the garden; the patient begins to
   write a diary for the doctor but other human contact is forbidden.

c. For a further week or two the patient is instructed to do heavier work, continue the diary, and attend lectures from the doctor on self-control, the evils of egocentricity, and so forth.

d. Finally, the patient gradually returns to full social life and his former occupation; the patient continues contact with the doctor and attends group sessions with other patients on an out-patient basis.

3. How do you think you would feel as a patient of Morita therapy?

4. Contrast Western psychotherapy and Morita therapy. How are they different?

5. Compare Western psychotherapy and Morita therapy. How are they the same?

6. Revise your definition of therapy to include both Morita therapy and Western psychotherapy. (*Hint*: focus on the *function* rather than the *process* of therapy.)

References:

Prince, R. (1980). Variations in psychotherapeutic procedures. In H. C. Triandis & J. Draguns (Eds.), *Handbook of cross-cultural psychology: Vol. 6. Psychopathology* (pp. 291-349). Boston: Allyn & Bacon.

Reynolds, D. K. (1976). *Morita therapy*. Berkeley, CA: University of California Press.

Chapter 7. Culture and Social Behavior

Name _____   Date _____

Activity 7.1
VIOLATING CULTURAL NORMS

Social norms are (often unspoken) rules or expectations about how people within a given group should behave. Social psychologists have found that people generally choose to conform to the social norms of the groups to which they belong. This activity explores the importance of the content and strength of social norms in defining a culture.

Directions: The statements below will instruct you to list social norms, choose one of these norms to violate, and then answer a series of questions based on your experience.

1. Examples of social norms relevant to some cultures include:

   • Forming a line when a group of people are waiting.

   • Applauding when a performance is completed.

   • Saying "excuse me" if you bump into strangers in a crowded place.

   In the spaces provided, list five social norms that you have observed.

   a.

   b.

   c.

   d.

   e.

2. Choose one of the norms you listed above to violate. Please be sure that your behavior is not illegal and does not put you or others in any danger. Your norm violation need not be anything very dramatic. Sometimes we can learn more by subtle than drastic norm violations.

In the space below, describe your violation of a social norm, including (a) the setting, (b) the nature of the norm violation, (c) how you felt during the norm violation, and (d) how others responded to your behavior.

Reactions:

1. Discuss the cultural value that underlies the norm you chose to violate.

2. Why do you think we generally conform to the social norms of our culture?

3. Why do you think we typically react negatively toward those who violate our social norms?

4. Have you ever inadvertently violated a social norm? Please explain.

5. How did you learn the social norms of your own culture?

6. How would you go about learning the social norms of an unfamiliar culture?

7. One of the dimensions used to make cross-cultural comparisons in Hofstede's (1980) classic study of employee responses in 40 nations is *uncertainty avoidance* (you may be familiar with another of the dimensions from this study -- individualism/ collectivism). Uncertainty avoidance refers to the degree to which efforts are made to avoid situations in which there are no clear expectations for behavior. Cultures that score high on uncertainty avoidance tend to have a greater amount and specificity of social norms. Hofstede found Greece, Japan, Mexico, and several South American and Central American countries to be high in uncertainty avoidance. Most Scandinavian and English speaking countries were low on uncertainty avoidance.

How might someone from a culture low in uncertainty avoidance experience life in a culture that is high in uncertainty avoidance? How do you think someone from a culture high in uncertainty avoidance might experience life in a culture that is low in uncertainty avoidance?

Reference:
    Hofstede, G. (1980). *Culture's consequences: International differences in work-related values*. Beverly Hills, CA: Sage.

Name _____   Date _____

Activity 7.2
THE TELECONDITIONING OF THE COLLEGE CLASSROOM

Social norms, a culture's rules or expectations about how people within a given group should behave, are not static. This activity will encourage you to think about the factors that influence change in social norms within a culture. More specifically, we will be focusing on how television viewing has affected social norms for behavior in the college classroom.

Conrad Kottak (1997) has proposed that extensive television viewing has resulted in the *teleconditioning* of Americans. That is, the development of behaviors associated with TV watching that are then manifested in nontelevision settings. Kottak suggests that teleconditioning has contributed to a variety of classroom behaviors including:

- talking while the class is ongoing
- eating or drinking in class
- reading (other than the course materials)
- casual posture (e.g., feet on chair or head on desk)
- walking in and out of a class that is in session
- leaving before the class is over
- couples engaging in intimate behavior during class

Directions: There are two parts to this activity. First, observe one or more college classes and note examples of teleconditioning. Choose a class other than the one in which this activity was assigned and be sure to check with someone enrolled in the class on the degree to which norms for classroom behavior are specified by the instructor (in the syllabus or otherwise). As Kottak points out, you may see more teleconditioning in larger classes where students tend to feel they are part of the "audience." Be sure to protect the identity of any individual students whose behavior you describe in this activity. The second part of this activity requires that you discuss your observations with someone who went to college (or taught college) at least 20 years ago and draw some conclusions about changes in classroom culture.

1. Describe the class(es) you observed including subject matter, class size, and instances of teleconditioned behavior among students (or instructors).

2. Discuss your observations with someone who went to college (or taught college) at least 20 years ago. Acknowledging that your observations are limited, what do you conclude about the degree to which college students have been teleconditioned?

3. Do you think you would find teleconditioned classroom behavior in all cultures in which television viewing is common? Why or why not?

4. Please describe another example (not involving television) of changing social norms in response to technology.

5. What other factors besides changes in technology might be involved in modifying social norms?

Reference:
    Kottak, C. P. (1997). Teleconditioning and the postmodern classroom. In J. Spradley & D. W. McCurdy (Eds.), *Conformity and conflict: Readings in cultural anthropology* (pp. 93-98). New York: Longman.

Name _____   Date _____

Activity 7.3
CULTURE AND ATTRIBUTION:
THE SELF-SERVING BIAS

In studies conducted in individualist cultures, Nisbett and Ross (1980) identified a tendency to attribute success to one's own skill (internal factors) and to attribute failure to aspects of the situation (external factors). Several cross-cultural psychologists have used evidence from collectivist cultures to challenge the universality of this tendency, called the *self-serving bias*. For example, Kashima and Triandis reported a *self-effacement bias* -- a tendency to attribute failures to lack of ability and success to situational factors -- in a study involving collectivist Japanese students. In a fascinating study (unrelated to the self-serving bias) conducted by Trafimow, Triandis, and Goto (1991), respondents from a collectivist culture were primed to think like individualists and respondents from an individualist culture were primed to think like collectivists. They found that both the respondent's cultural background and the instructions given influenced the nature of their responses. In this activity we will explore the effect of cultural background and priming to see how they influence attributions for success and failure.

Directions: You will need to request the assistance of four volunteers for this activity. Each of the participants will write a brief story in response to slightly different instructions. Formulate predictions about the responses of the participants using the chart below. Then, collect responses from all four participants and code the attributions for success and failure using the descriptions of internal and external attributions. Finally, answer the reaction questions on the last page of this activity.

Predicted attributions: Based on the instructions given to the four participants (ignoring their actual cultural background) predict below whether each participant would be likely to make internal or external attributions.

	Instructions	
Outcome	Individualist	Collectivist
Success	Participant A	Participant B
Failure	Participant C	Participant D

Participant A _____   Participant C _____

Participant B _____   Participant D _____

Participant A

First, spend a few minutes thinking about yourself as an individual who is separate and distinct from your friends and family. Then, in the space provided below, write a brief account of an experience in which you successfully achieved a goal or completed a task.

Participant B

First, spend a few minutes thinking about how you are similar to and connected with your friends and family. Then, in the space provided below, write a brief account of an experience in which you successfully achieved a goal or completed a task.

Participant C

First, spend a few minutes thinking about yourself as an individual who is separate and distinct from your friends and family. Then, in the space provided below, write a brief account of an experience in which you failed to achieve a goal or complete a task.

Participant D

First, spend a few minutes thinking about how you are similar to and connected with your friends and family. Then, in the space provided below, write a brief account of an experience in which you failed to achieve a goal or complete a task.

Coding Attributions:

Internal attributions focus on ability, effort, emotions, personality traits, or personal preferences.

External attributions focus on luck, fate, economic circumstances, task difficulty, or the actions of others.

Reactions:

1. Based on the descriptions of internal and external attributions above, indicate the primary form of attributions used by each participant.

Participant A _____   Participant C _____

Participant B _____   Participant D _____

2. To what extent were your predictions supported by your data?

3. Did the participants' actual cultural background (in terms of individualism and collectivism) have a greater impact on their responses than did the individualist or collectivist priming in the instructions? Please explain.

4. Based on your data, what do you conclude about the universality of the self-serving bias?

References:

   Kashima, Y., & Triandis, H. C. (1986). The self-serving bias in attributions as a coping strategy: A cross-cultural study, *Journal of Cross-Cultural Psychology, 17*, 83-97.

   Nisbett, R. E., & Ross, L. (1980). *Human inference: Strategies and shortcomings of social judgments.* Englewood Cliffs, NJ: Prentice Hall.

   Trafimow, D., Triandis, H. C., & Goto, S. G. (1991). Some tests of the distinction between private self and the collective self. *Journal of Personality and Social Psychology, 60*, 649-655.

Name _____   Date _____

Activity 7.4
ANALYZING INSULTS

G. R. Semin and Monica Rubini (1990) compared insults produced by residents of Catania (a collectivist region of southern Italy), Trieste (an individualist region of northern Italy), and Bologna (a region that is not strongly individualist or collectivist in central Italy). One of their findings was that people from the southern collectivist region produced more insults that targeted a person and his or her relations than did people from the northern individualist region. Insults produced by people in the central region were intermediate in terms of these relational insults. The purpose of this activity is to explore the use of insults as an indicator of individualism and collectivism.

Directions: For this activity you will need to find three different people to produce insults for you. Use the interview format below to collect the insults and to determine whether your interviewee comes from a more individualist or collectivist background. Remember that the dimension of individualism and collectivism is generally used as a *country-level variable*. Specific people may be collectivist (called *allocentric* as a person-level variable) or individualist (called *idiocentric* as a person-level variable) regardless of whether they reside in a collectivist or individualist nation. Once you have collected the insults using the interview format, use Semin and Rubini's coding categories below to sort the insults into individualist and collectivist (relational) responses. Then answer the questions that follow.

Coding Categories: (These categories are adapted from Semin and Rubini's, 1990 research *in Italy*. You may need to add or modify items in these categories in order to fit the cultural context.)

Individualist Insults:
- Insults involving denial of psychological properties (such as calling someone an idiot).
- Insults involving denial of physical features or health (such as calling someone ugly or wishing them illness).
- Insults regarding civil conduct (such as insults referring to a lack of manners).
- Insults involving references to the boundaries between the normal and the abnormal, such as analogies between the insulted person and animals (for example, calling someone a pig) or references to excretia or dirtiness.
- Insults concerning sexual organs or activities.

Collectivist (Relational) Insults:
- Insults referring to incestuous acts
- Sexual insults directed to the target person *and* his or her relatives (such as calling someone a "bastard.")
- Insults implying bad wishes to the target person *as well as* his or her relatives.
- Sexual insults directed to persons related to the target.
- Insults implying that one's relative resembles an animal.
- Insults referring to group membership (such as ethnic slurs).

Swear Words (not individualist or collectivist)
- Swear words involving religious figures.
- Swear words referring to sexual nouns.

Interview Format

Participant A

Please state three to five different things you could say to insult someone.

Participant B

Please state three to five different things you could say to insult someone.

Participant C

Please state three to five different things you could say to insult someone.

Reactions:

1. Did you observe any association between the type of insult (individualist/collectivist) and the cultural context in the data you collected?

2. Semin and Rubini suggest that type of insult may vary with social class. Would you expect more relational insults among lower or higher income groups? Please explain.

3. Semin and Rubini suggest that insults are generally used within the context of blame and conflict over responsibility. Why then might collectivist cultures use more relational insults than individualist cultures in such a context?

4. Bond and Venus (1991) conducted a study of insults targeting participants from the Chinese University of Hong Kong. In one part of this study, these authors found less resistance to an individual insult (e.g., "You are stupid.") than a group insult (e.g. "You are stupid and I suspect all members of your department are stupid too!") Would these findings support or contradict Semin and Rubini's findings? Please explain.

Source:
    Insult categories adapted from Semin, G. R., & Rubini, M. Unfolding the concept of person by verbal abuse. *European Journal of Social Psychology, 20*, 463-474. Copyright (c) 1990 by John Wiley & Sons, Ltd. Adapted with permission.

References:
    Bond, M., & Venus, C. K. (1991). Resistance to group or personal insults in an ingroup or outgroup context. *International Journal of Psychology, 26*, 83-94.
    Semin, G. R., & Rubini, M. (1990). Unfolding the concept of person by verbal abuse. *European Journal of Social Psychology, 20*, 463-474.

Name _____   Date _____

Activity 7.5
AGGRESSION ACROSS CULTURES: A SELF-QUIZ

This activity explores some of the factors that may help us to understand cross-cultural variation in rates of aggressive behavior.

Directions: Decide whether each of the statements below is true or false. Then check your answers on page 381.

1. A very small number of societies are free of aggression.   TRUE / FALSE

2. Across cultures, males are more physically and verbally
   aggressive than females.   TRUE / FALSE

3. Violence in the media predicts a violent society.   TRUE / FALSE

4. In cultures where aggression is repressed, it is ultimately
   expressed in destructive ways.   TRUE / FALSE

5. A high level of violent behavior tends to be present in
   countries characterized by a "frontier mentality."   TRUE / FALSE

6. In the United States, one of the few industrialized nations
   practicing capital punishment, there is a negative correlation
   between the number of executions and the murder rate
   (that is, when the rate of executions increases, the murder
   rate decreases).   TRUE / FALSE

7. One of the best predictors of a country's homicide rate is the
   availability of firearms.   TRUE / FALSE

8. Across cultures studied, parental rejection is a strong
   predictor of children's violence.   TRUE / FALSE

9. People from the northern United States are more likely than
   people from the southern United States to react to insults
   with violence.   TRUE / FALSE

10. Societies that have more war also tend to have more
    warlike sports.   TRUE / FALSE

Name _____   Date _____

Activity 7.6
AN INTERCULTURAL CONFLICT

Over the past decade there has been an increased effort to apply findings from cross-cultural research to the theory and practice of conflict resolution. Researchers have studied how cultural differences may impact perceptions of the process as well as the content of disputes. For example, Stella Ting-Toomey's (1988) face-negotiation theory addresses cultural differences in the *process* of conflict resolution. Her research indicates that members of individualistic cultures tend to use more direct methods of conflict management, whereas members of more collectivistic cultures use more indirect methods of handling conflict. Ting-Toomey suggests that the less direct styles typically used by collectivists enables both parties to "save face."

Bradford 'J' Hall and Mutsumi Noguchi (1993) have addressed the *content* of intercultural disputes. These authors focus on the *kernel images* or key symbols involved in a dispute that may have varied meanings depending on the cultural context. In this activity we will explore the role of cultural differences in both the content of a dispute and the process of conflict resolution in a simulation based on a case study documented by Hall and Noguchi (1993) and Ting-Toomey's (1988) model of conflict styles. The critical kernel image in this conflict is that of the dolphin.

Directions: Find two of your friends who are willing to act out a brief role play. After reading both parts yourself, assign one of your friends to the part of the Iki Fishermen's Representative and the other to the part of the Conservationists' Representative. Ask them to read the directions and then take part in a simulated negotiation based on the information they have been given. Be sure that the participants do not read each other's information sheets. Please take careful notes about the interaction so that you can more fully complete the questions at the end of this activity. Do not intervene in the simulated conflict negotiations unless the participants are at a standstill or are losing sight of the fact that this is only a simulation!

Iki Fishermen's Representative

Directions: After you read the information below, you will be involved in a simulated negotiation with an individual playing the part of the Conservationists' Representative. Please do not change any of the facts of the case stated below. Feel free, however, to use your creativity to elaborate on these facts. You may introduce the information stated below into your negotiation as you see fit. Whenever possible, please use the negotiation style specified below.

Background Information:

- The crisis began when the arrival of a large number of dolphin in the waters surrounding the Japanese island of Iki was accompanied by a dramatic decrease in fishing output.

- In 1978, a report on Japanese TV documented the slaughter of over one thousand dolphins by the fishermen of Iki Island. The report was soon broadcast worldwide, resulting in shock and outrage in the West.

- Following the broadcast, several Western conservationists approached the Iki fishermen to discuss options for resolving the situation.

- The conservationists tried unsuccessfully to convince the fishermen that the dolphins were not responsible for the decrease in fishing output.

- When no agreement was initially reached, some conservationists took matters into their own hands, secretly freeing dolphins from the nets of the Iki fishermen.

Iki Fishermen's Perspective:

- We are faced with a choice between standing by and losing our entire way of life or fighting to preserve our families, our community, and our livelihood.

- We were the ones who initially invited the Japanese reporters to cover the dolphin killings. We were trying to convey the gravity of our situation to our government so that they would provide assistance. However, our plea was intercepted by outsiders.

- The conservationists lack compassion and are incapable of understanding the plight of our people and the heroic battle we are waging.

- We view the *iruka* or dolphin as an evil creature, the gangster of the sea, the enemy of the fishermen.

- We use the term *iruka*, which means "sea pig" because, until the mid-1800s dolphins were a primary source of protein for the Japanese people. Prior to that time, Buddhist tenets prohibited the consumption of four-legged animals.

- The dolphins killed at Iki were not eaten by people, but were used as fertilizer and pig food.

- In day-to-day discussion, we often substitute words such as *enemies*, *competitors*, *criminals*, or *gangsters* for the word *dolphin*.

Negotiation Style:
- Directness and contradiction are avoided.

- Much of what is communicated is done so indirectly, through nuance, nonverbals, or in what is *not said*.

- Allowing members of the negotiation to maintain face or respect is critical.

- Expressions of respect and courtesy are important.

- The relationship between disputants must be mended if the conflict is to be resolved.

- Conflict typically involves violations of one's sense of group loyalty or ingroup/outgroup boundaries.

- It is important to recognize the historical roots of current conflicts.

- Silences are natural and useful.

Conservationists' Representative

Directions: After you read the information below, you will be involved in a simulated negotiation with an individual playing the part of the Iki Fishermen's Representative. Please do not change any of the facts of the case stated below. Feel free, however, to use your creativity to elaborate on these facts. You may introduce the information stated below into your negotiation as you see fit. Whenever possible, please use the negotiation style specified below.

Background Information:
- The crisis began when the arrival of a large number of dolphin in the waters surrounding the Japanese island of Iki was accompanied by a dramatic decrease in fishing output.

- In 1978, a report on Japanese TV documented the slaughter of over one thousand dolphins by the fishermen of Iki Island. The report was soon broadcast worldwide, resulting in shock and outrage in the West.

- Following the broadcast, several Western conservationists approached the Iki fishermen to discuss options for resolving the situation.

- The conservationists tried unsuccessfully to convince the fishermen that the dolphins were not responsible for the decrease in fishing output.

- When no agreement was initially reached, some conservationists took matters into their own hands, secretly freeing dolphins from the nets of the Iki fishermen.

Conservationists' Perspective:
- We are concerned with the rights and freedom of all beings.

- The Japanese fishermen don't really understand the ecological situation. We have tried to make it clear to them that dolphins are not the cause of their declining catch.

- Concern with the lack of an agreement and the continued drift-net fishing on the part of the Japanese has led to heroic efforts by some of our side, risking their lives to free hundreds of dolphins under cover of darkness.

- Dolphins are endangered.

- Dolphins are highly intelligent and friendly animals that have a special bond with humans (as in the "Flipper" television series).

- The Western image of dolphins has its roots in Greek mythology in which the special status of dolphins allowed them to communicate with the Gods.

- The concept of killing, and particularly eating, dolphins is repulsive to us.

Negotiation Style:
- Directness and confrontation are admirable.

- Conflict is dysfunctional if it is suppressed.

- The relationship between individuals involved in a dispute should be separate from "the issues."

- Conflict typically involves violations of one's sense of power, autonomy, or fairness.

- It is important to justify one's position and build up credibility.

- Bringing up the historical roots of current conflicts is generally a waste of time.

- Silences are uncomfortable.

Reactions:

1. How did the participants react to the differences in negotiation style?

2. How did differences in "kernal image" enter into this dispute?

3. Were the participants able to negotiate a resolution? If so, what strategies were helpful in coming to agreement? If not, what obstacles impeded the resolution of this dispute?

4. Were cultural differences in content or process directly discussed by the participants? If so, how was this accomplished? If not, do you think making the cultural differences explicit would have been helpful?

5. Do you think a third party (mediator) might have facilitated the resolution of this dispute? Please explain.

Source:

   Simulation adapted from Hall, B. J., & Noguchi, M. Intercultural conflict: A case study. *International Journal of Intercultural Relations, 17,* 399-413. Copyright (c) 1993 by Elsevier Science. Adapted with permission.

References:

   Hall, B. J., & Noguchi, M. (1993). Intercultural conflict: A case study. *International Journal of Intercultural Relations, 17,* 399-413.

   Ting-Toomey, S. (1988). Intercultural conflict styles: A face-negotiation theory. In Y. Y. Kim & W. GudyKunst (Eds.), *Theories in intercultural communication* (pp. 213-235). Newbury Park, CA: Sage.

Name _____   Date _____

Activity 7.7
WORK-RELATED VALUES

The basis of much cross-cultural research in -- and outside of -- the workplace is Geert Hofstede's (1980) research on work-related values. Hofstede studied the values of International Business Machines (IBM) employees in over 50 countries. Based on this data he derived four dimensions of cultural variability: individualism-collectivism, power distance, uncertainty avoidance, and masculinity-femininity. Hofstede used the average scores of workers in each country to rank countries on each of the four dimensions. More recently, a group of researchers known as the Chinese Culture Connection (1987) identified a fifth value, Confucian Work Dynamism. The purpose of this activity is to better understand these five dimensions by applying them to a workplace with which you are familiar.

Directions: First write a brief description of a work setting with which you are familiar. Then read the descriptions of the five dimensions below and in the questions that follow apply the dimensions to your work setting.

Workplace Description (include type of business or occupation, approximate number of employees, and structure in terms of managers and subordinates):

Work-Related Values

As compared to Individualistic cultures, cultures high in Collectivism tend to be characterized by:
- a focus on the goals of the group rather than individual goals
- achievement attributed to the efforts of the group rather than the individual
- avoidance of confrontation
- the perception that direct requests are an ineffective form of communication
- working in groups

Cultures high in Power Distance tend to be characterized by:
- clear distinctions between superiors and subordinates
- the acceptance of unequal power distribution
- dependence of subordinates on superiors
- conformity
- unquestioning compliance with the orders of superiors

Cultures high in Uncertainty Avoidance tend to be characterized by:
- lower tolerance for ambiguity
- greater need for consensus
- greater need for formal rules
- avoidance of conflict
- resistance to change

As compared to Feminine cultures, cultures high in Masculinity are characterized by:
- a high value on things as opposed to people
- a focus on power and competition as opposed to nurturance
- the perception that work is central to one's life
- an emphasis on distinct gender roles

Cultures high in Confucian Work Dynamism tend to be characterized by:
- organizations modeled after the structure of the family
- thrift
- patience and perseverance
- having a sense of shame

Reactions:

1. Would you describe this workplace as characterized more by individualism or collectivism? Please explain.

2. Would you describe this workplace as having high, moderate, or low power distance? Please explain.

3. Would you describe this workplace as having high, moderate, or low uncertainty avoidance? Please explain.

4. Would you describe this workplace as characterized more by masculinity or femininity? Please explain.

5. Is this workplace characterized by aspects of Confucian Work Dynamism? Please explain.

6. Are the values manifested in this workplace characteristic of the dominant culture? Please explain.

7. Are the values manifested in this workplace conducive to a diverse workforce? Please explain.

References:
    Chinese Culture Connection. (1987). Chinese values and the search for culture-free dimensions of culture. *Journal of Cross-Cultural Psychology, 18*, 143-164.
    Hofstede, G. (1980). *Culture's consequences: International differences in work-related values.* Newbury Park, CA: Sage.

Name _____   Date _____

Activity 7.8
LEADERSHIP STYLES

A major interest of those who study organizational behavior has focused on how to select and train effective leaders. Issues of leadership become an even greater concern when it involves international businesses or organizations within a country that have diverse workforces. This activity explores cultural variability in the concept of leadership.

Directions: Spend a few minutes thinking about your image of a leader. Then complete the five sentences below to describe characteristics of a good leader and answer the questions that follow.

- A good leader _____.
- A good leader _____.
- A good leader _____.
- A good leader _____.
- A good leader _____.

A large number of studies of organizational behavior are based on a model that categorizes leadership style along two dimensions: concern for task or production and concern for relationships or people (for example, Blake & Mouton, 1964). There is significant evidence that forms of these two dimensions can be used to describe leadership behavior across cultures and that across cultures workers tend to prefer leaders that exhibit both task-oriented and relationship-oriented behaviors (Hui & Luk, 1997). Indian managers have been described as both task- and relationship-oriented. J. B. P. Sinha (1980) described the Indian manager as a nurturant task leader, who acts toward the employees as a parent would toward a child. Treating each subordinate fairly, then, does not mean treating them all the same, but making sure that the needs of each are met to the extent possible. As these needs differ, so will the treatment. According to Sinha, leadership in the businesses of India involves more participation in the projects of subordinates rather than merely giving instructions as to which tasks are to be undertaken. Furthermore, there is not the distinction between work and personal life that one finds in the United States and Canada. The manager is expected to provide advice and at times intervene if an employee is experiencing problems unrelated to work. For example, a manager in India may select a marriage partner for an employee or provide guidance in family disputes.

1. Would a person having the five characteristics you listed above make an effective leader in the Indian context Sinha describes? If not, what other characteristics would be important?

2. Ling, Chen, and Wang (1987) have suggested that in addition to attending to task and relationship, good leaders in China must have an additional quality -- strong moral character. To what extent is moral character a component of leadership in your culture? Please explain.

3. Look back at your list of the characteristics of a good leader. Would you consider most of those traits to be more masculine or more feminine? Please explain.

4. Studies of gender and leadership (conducted primarily among white women in the United States) find little difference between the leadership styles of women and men. However, there is evidence that supports the idea that women who use a more task-oriented style are evaluated (particulary by males) more harshly than men who use a task-oriented style (see for example, Rojahn & Willemsen, 1994). How might you explain these findings? What are the implications of these findings for women in the workforce?

5. Gerstner and Day (1994) had participants from eight countries rate a list of 59 attributes according to the degree to which each fit their image of a business leader. This study found that the trait *goal oriented* appeared most consistently and was rated highly by members of six cultures. Among various cultural differences identified in this study, *verbal skills* were emphasized by participants from France and the United States; and not by participants from Germany, Honduras, India, Taiwan, China, or Japan. How might you explain this finding?

6. Based on your work in this activity, draw some conclusions about the characteristics of an effective leader.

References:

Blake, R. R., & Mouton, J. S. (1964). *The managerial grid*. Houston: Gulf.

Gerstner, C. R., & Day, D. V. (1994). Cross-cultural comparison of leadership prototypes. *Leadership Quarterly, 5*, 121-134.

Hui, C. H., & Luk, C. L. (1997). Industrial/organizational psychology. In J. W. Berry, M. H. Segall, & C. Kagitcibasi (Eds.), *Handbook of cross-cultural psychology: Vol 3. Social behavior and applications.* (2nd ed., pp. 371-411), Boston: Allyn & Bacon.

Ling, W. Q., Chen, L., & Wang, D. (1987). Construction of CPM scale for leadership behavior assessment. *Acta Psychologica Sinica, 3*, 236-242.

Rojahn, K., & Willemsen, T. M. (1994). The evaluation of gender-role congruent and gender-role incongruent leaders. *SexRoles, 30*(1-2), 109-119.

Sinha, J. B. P. (1980). *The nurturant task leader*. New Delhi, India: Sage.

Name _____   Date _____

Activity 7.9
LOVE AND MARRIAGE

This activity explores cultural differences in beliefs about love and marriage. Once you have completed this activity, you should have a better understanding of the cultural context of your own beliefs about love and marriage.

Directions: Robert Levine and colleagues (1995) asked college students in 11 cultures (India, Pakistan, Thailand, Mexico, Brazil, Japan, Hong Kong, Republic of the Philippines, Australia, England, and the United States) to complete the questions below. First, answer these questions based on your own beliefs. Then respond to the reaction questions that follow in order to better understand the cultural influences on your beliefs.

The questions below ask for your thoughts about marriage. Since only heterosexual couples may legally marry in most parts of the world, you may also think about these questions in terms of making a lifelong commitment.

1. If a man (woman) had all the other qualities you desired, would you marry this person if you were not in love with him (her)?

No _____   Yes _____

Please explain:

2. If love has completely disappeared from a marriage, I think it is probably best for the couple to make a clean break and start new lives.

Agree _____   Disagree _____

Please explain:

3. In my opinion, the disappearance of love is not a sufficient reason for ending a marriage and should not be viewed as such.

Agree _____   Disagree _____

Please explain:

Reactions:
1. Levine and colleagues found that members of individualistic cultures were more likely than members of collectivistic cultures to view love as important in decisions about marriage. In fact, in some collectivist cultures, intense romantic love is viewed as immature and threatening to the family structure. How might you explain this finding?

2. Levine and colleagues also reported a distinction among collectivist cultures, with members of more economically developed countries (such as Japan and Hong Kong) attributing greater importance to love than less economically developed collectivist cultures (such as India, Pakistan, Thailand, and the Phillipines). How might you explain this finding?

3. In a 1967 study of American college students, Kephart reported that 65 % of males and 24 % of females answered "no" to the question about marrying someone who had the qualities you desired, but with whom you are not in love. No such gender differences were found by Levine and colleagues. Approximately 80 % of males and females in their sample of Americans answered "no" to the same question. How might you explain the dramatic change in response of American females between 1967 and 1995? Why do you think the scores of males show increased importance attributed to love over that same period of time?

4. What concerns might you have about the methodology of a study, such as that of Levine and colleagues, that makes cross-cultural comparisons of college students?

5. What cultural messages may have influenced your own beliefs about the importance of love in marriage or lifelong commitments?

Sources:
    Adapted from Kephart, W. M. (1967). Some correlates of romantic love. *Journal of Marriage and the Family, 29,* 470-474, and
    Levine, R., Sato, S., Hashimoto, T., & Verma, J. (1995). Love and marriage in eleven cultures. *Journal of Cross-Cultural Psychology, 26,* 554-571.

Name _____ Date _____

Activity 7.10
INTERCULTURAL PARTNERSHIPS

The frequency of intercultural romantic partnerships is increasing rapidly in many parts of the world. Early writing on intercultural relationships focused on pathological motivation for entering into these unions, such as rebelling against one's own culture or even unconscious hatred of one's opposite sex parent (and thus choosing a partner who does not physically resemble him or her!). We now know that most people enter intercultural relationships for the same reasons most people enter intracultural (same culture) relationships: warmth, love, affection, excitement, caring, intimacy, and solidarity (Jeter, 1982). In fact, people in enduring intercultural partnerships may even have or develop some special skills for dealing with cultural differences. This activity will allow you to explore some of the challenges and adaptations of people in intercultural relationships.

Directions: For this activity you are to interview someone who is involved in an intercultural dating relationship, marriage, or committed partnership.

Select a respondent. It is up to you to determine what constitutes "intercultural" here. Researchers of intercultural relationships have focused primarily on individuals who differ in terms of race/ethnicity, religion, and nationality. For this activity, however, you may define intercultural more broadly.

Check for time constraints. Reserve at least 15 minutes for the interview.

Obtain informed consent. Explain the purpose of the interview (to explore the challenges of intercultural partnerships) and be sure that your respondent understands that his or her responses may be discussed in class or included in a written report.

Assure and maintain confidentiality. Be sure you tell your respondent that you will not in any way attach his or her name to the responses in reporting or discussing the responses to the interview. It is critical that you maintain this confidentiality in order to conduct the interview in an ethical manner.

Conduct the interview. Ask the interview questions in the order in which they appear in this activity. Be sure to take notes in the space provided or on a separate sheet.

Summarize the interview data for each respondent and then complete the reactions section of this activity.

Provide feedback to the respondent if appropriate. If you have some general conclusions about intercultural relationships based on discussing or analyzing the interview data with your class you might convey these conclusions to your respondents. Be sure to thank him or her for the time they spent assisting you with this exercise.

Interview Format

1. In what way is your relationship with your partner an *intercultural* relationship? Please explain.

2. Please describe one or two cultural differences that have affected your relationship with your partner.

3. Please describe the *most* useful strategy you have used in dealing with cultural differences in your relationship.

4. Please describe the *least* useful strategy you have used in dealing with cultural differences in your relationship.

5. As a couple, do you spend more time with individuals from your own cultural background, from your partner's cultural background, or neither. Please explain how this has affected your relationship.

6. Have you learned any skills, as a result of being in an intercultural relationship, that would assist you in other types of intercultural situations?

Reactions:

1. The list below is adapted from Dugan Romano's (1997) work on common challenges for intercultural couples. Circle any of these challenges that seem to characterize the relationship of your interviewee.

a. values	g. friends	m. response to stress
b. food and drink	h. finances	n. conflict-handling style
c. politics	i. partner's family	o. response to illness
d. male-female roles	j. social class	p. sexual behavior
e. time	k. religion	q. communication or
f. place of residence	l. raising children	language

Please explain how your interviewee is faced by the challenges you indicated.

2. Discuss what you have learned from this interview about effective and ineffective strategies for intercultural interaction.

3. Romano (1997) describes four types for understanding intercultural marriages, labeled Submission/Immersion, Obliteration, Compromise, and Consensus. After reading the explanations of each of these types, decide which best fits the circumstances of your interviewee.

Submission/Immersion: One partner virtually abandons his or her own culture while immersing him- or herself in the culture of the other partner.

Obliteration: The couple forms a new third culture identity, maintaining none of the practices of their original cultures and thus eliminating all cultural differences.

Compromise: Each partner gives up some (often important) aspects of his or her own culture to allow for the other's cultural practices or beliefs.

Consensus: The couple makes an ongoing search for solutions in which neither partner sacrifices aspects of culture essential to his or her well-being. Partners allow each other to be different without viewing difference as threatening.

Which (if any) of the four types above best characterizes the relationship of your interviewee? Please explain.

4. Put an 'X' in the blank to indicate which of the following relationships you would consider to be intercultural (assume each difference stated below is the only major difference between partners).

_____ a. One partner is Swiss; the other is Chilean.

_____ b. One partner is Buddhist; the other is Christian.

_____ c. One partner is wealthy; the other is middle class.

_____ d. One partner is deaf; the other is hearing.

_____ e. One partner is a first generation Korean immigrant; the other is a third generation Korean immigrant.

_____ f. One partner comes from a rural area; the other partner comes from an urban area (of the same country).

_____ g. One partner is male; the other is female.

5. Based on the items that you indicated above and on your interview data, write a definition of intercultural partnership.

6. Look back to the list of challenges in question 1 of the Reactions section of this activity. Which of the challenges are unique to intercultural relationships and would not be relevant to intracultural relationships?

References:
   Jeter, K. (1982). Analytic essay: Intercultural and interracial marriage. *Marriage and Family Review, 5,* 105-111.
   Romano, D. (1997). *Intercultural marriage: Promises and pitfalls* (2nd ed.). Yarmouth, ME: Intercultural Press.

Chapter 8. Intergroup Relations

Name _____   Date _____

Activity 8.1
DISCRIMINATION INCIDENTS

Discrimination has been defined as "negative behaviors directed toward members of socially defined groups because they are members of this group" (Stephan & Stephan, 1996, p. 35).   A large number of psychological studies have examined the characteristics of people who engage in discriminatory behavior. We know, for example, that an individual's level of prejudice tends not to be a good predictor of whether he or she will discriminate (Ajzen & Fishbein, 1977). Only recently have psychologists begun to explore the effect of discrimination on the target of such actions (see, for example, Swim & Stangor, 1998). This activity is designed to encourage you to think about what constitutes discrimination, why it occurs, and its effects on the target of discrimination.

Directions: In the space provided below, please write an account of an incident of discrimination that you either experienced, witnessed, or were told about. Then answer the questions on the following pages.

Reactions:

1. How did you (or the person involved) feel as the target of discrimination?

2. Who is privileged by this form of discrimination?

3. What may have led to this behavior on the part of the individual(s) who discriminated?

4. Is it possible to explain this event without acknowledging that discrimination took place?

5. How could this form of discrimination be prevented?

References:

Ajzen, I., & Fishbein, M. (1977). Attitude-behavior relations: A theoretical analysis and a review of the empirical research. *Psychological Bulletin, 84*, 888-918.

Stephan, W. G., & Stephan, C. W. (1996). *Intergroup relations*. Boulder, CO: Westview.

Swim, J. K., & Stangor, C. (1998). *Prejudice: The target's perspective*. San Diego, CA: Academic Press.

Name _____   Date _____

Activity 8.2
EXPLORING PRIVILEGE

Although most of us readily acknowledge the discrimination that exists in our societies, we often have difficulty recognizing the forms of unearned privilege that are the counterpart of discrimination. For example, imagine that a White woman and a Black woman walk into a clothing store at the same time. There are several unoccupied salespeople in the store. One salesperson rushes to assist the White customer. No one assists the Black customer. We can easily understand that the Black customer is the target of discrimination. What may be more difficult to understand is that the White customer is the recipient of an unearned privilege. This activity will help you explore this concept of privilege and understand how you as an individual may or may not be privileged.

Directions: For each of the categories below, read the example and write a second statement that illustrates the form of privilege specified.

1. White skin privilege:
[Example: I can be pretty sure that hiring decisions will be based on my skills and experience.]

2. Male privilege:
[Example: I can order a large meal at a restaurant without feeling self-conscious.]

3. Heterosexual privilege:
[Example: I can freely introduce my significant other to family or coworkers.]

4. Ablebodied privilege:
[Example: I can ask for directions without being treated as though I am mentally impaired.]

5. Middle class privilege:
[Example: If I become ill, I can be confident that I will receive the medical treatment I need.]

6. What other forms of privilege exist? Identify one additional form of privilege and write a statement illustrating that form of privilege below.

Reactions:
1. Most people have not given much thought to the forms of privilege they experience. Why do you think we are relatively unaware of the privileges we receive?

2. Do you think that once we are aware of one form of privilege we are better able to understand other forms of privilege? Why or why not?

3. To what extent is an understanding of privilege relevant to eliminating discrimination? Please explain.

4. How can people become more aware of the ways in which they are privileged?

Name _____   Date _____

Activity 8.3
INSTITUTIONAL DISCRIMINATION

The term *institutional racism* was first used by Stokely Carmichael and Charles V. Hamilton in their 1967 book, *Black Power*. They used this term to distinguish between the racist behavior of *individuals* and the policies and practices of *institutions* that perpetuate racism. Institutional discrimination is not limited to issues of race, but includes the systematic perpetuation of other forms of inequality as well. This activity explores the concept of institutional discrimination; that is, policies or practices of organizations that *systematically* privilege members of some groups and discriminate against members of other groups.

Directions: For each of the policies below, determine whether it is a form of institutional discrimination. If you find it is, then please answer the additional questions following each policy.

1. Children of alumni receive preference for admission into some colleges and universities.

    a. This is institutional discrimination: Yes _____ No _____

    b. Against which groups, if any, might this policy discriminate?

    c. What is the purpose of this policy?

    d. If this purpose is a valid one, how else might it be achieved?

2. An employment agency advertises for an "All-American type" to fill a public relations position.

    a. This is institutional discrimination: Yes _____ No _____

b. Against which groups, if any, might this policy discriminate?

c. What is the purpose of this policy?

d. If this purpose is a valid one, how else might it be achieved?

3. A pubic meeting is held on the third floor of a building without elevators.

a. This is institutional discrimination: Yes _____   No _____

b. Against which groups, if any, might this policy discriminate?

c. What is the purpose of this policy?

d. If this purpose is a valid one, how else might it be achieved?

4. A corporation decides to fill a position opening "in-house" rather than advertise.

a. This is institutional discrimination: Yes _____   No _____

b. Against which groups, if any, might this policy discriminate?

c. What is the purpose of this policy?

d. If this purpose is a valid one, how else might it be achieved?

5. The YWCA/YMCA offers a reduced family membership rate.

a. This is institutional discrimination: Yes _____ No _____

b. Against which groups, if any, might this policy discriminate?

c. What is the purpose of this policy?

d. If this purpose is a valid one, how else might it be achieved?

6. Persons accused of a crime who cannot post bail are imprisoned and thus may appear in court dressed in prison garb.

a. This is institutional discrimination: Yes _____ No _____

b. Against which groups, if any, might this policy discriminate?

c. What is the purpose of this policy?

d. If this purpose is a valid one, how else might it be achieved?

7. A Caucasian actor is chosen to play the part of an Asian man.

a. This is institutional discrimination: Yes _____ No _____

b. Against which groups, if any, might this policy discriminate?

c. What is the purpose of this policy?

d. If this purpose is a valid one, how else might it be achieved?

8. A teacher requires an oral presentation as part of the final grade.

a. This is institutional discrimination: Yes _____ No _____

b. Against which groups, if any, might this policy discriminate?

c. What is the purpose of this policy?

d. If this purpose is a valid one, how else might it be achieved?

9. An employee of a particular university is allowed free tuition as is his or her spouse.

a. This is institutional discrimination: Yes _____ No _____

b. Against which groups, if any, might this policy discriminate?

c. What is the purpose of this policy?

d. If this purpose is a valid one, how else might it be achieved?

10. A fire department requires that applicants for the position of firefighter be of a minimum height.

a. This is institutional discrimination: Yes _____ No _____

b. Against which groups, if any, might this policy discriminate?

c. What is the purpose of this policy?

d. If this purpose is a valid one, how else might it be achieved?

Reference:
    Carmichael, S., & Hamilton, C. V. (1967). *Black power: The politics of liberation in America.* New York: Vintage Books.

Name _____   Date _____

Activity 8.4
MARGINALITY AND PRIVILEGE ON A COLLEGE CAMPUS

Colleges and universities in many parts of the world are experiencing shifts in the demographic makeup of their student body. Helen Roberts and colleagues (1994, p. 20), for example, have written about the "myth of the 'typical' college student" in the United States. They note increasing diversity in terms of the age, gender, ethnicity, social class, and immigrant status of the college population. Roberts and colleagues suggest, however, that the college curriculum and programming have not kept pace with these changes. This activity will allow you to explore some of the ways in which a disregard for diversity is institutionalized in an educational setting.

Directions: In the space provided below, describe a college campus in which a traditionally marginalized group is, instead, privileged. Include in your description admissions and hiring practices, physical layout, curriculum, and extracurricular activities. Be sure not to base your design on stereotypes of the group you are privileging.

- **Example:** A campus in which wheelchair users are privileged might include such characteristics as: (1) architectural accessibility to wheelchairs with ceilings and doorways wheelchair height, and classrooms with open floor space. The TABS, or "temporarily able bodied" could make special arrangements in advance to have chairs in class; (2) extracurricular clubs oriented toward wheelchair activities, though the TABs have a small support group "The Coalition to End TABophobia"; (3) textbooks that generally picture people using wheelchairs, with the exception of those who are deviant in terms of mental health or criminal activity; and (4) a curriculum focused on the experiences of those in wheelchairs. For example, there might be a history course that chronicles achievements of individuals who use wheelchairs, though it does include a special unit for "TAB History Week."

1. Describe the group you have chosen to privilege.

2. Describe the admissions and hiring practices, physical layout, curriculum, and extracurricular activities of the college campus.

Reference:
   Roberts, H., Gonzales, J. C., Harris, O. D., Huff, D. J., Johns, A. M., Lou, R., & Scott, O. L. (1994). *Teaching from a multicultural perspective*. Thousand Oaks, CA: Sage.

Name _____   Date _____

Activity 8.5
LEARNING TO BE PREJUDICED

We often assume that children learn forms of prejudice primarily from their parents. Recent research on racial attitudes indicates enormous variability in the degree to which children's beliefs parallel those of their parents (see for example, Rohan & Zanna, 1996). What other factors in addition to the views expressed by family members might contribute to prejudicial beliefs? This activity will help you to think through some of the early influences on our beliefs about others who differ from ourselves in terms of such categories as race, ethnicity, social class, disability, religion, and sexual orientation.

Directions:
Select two respondents. For this activity you will need to recruit two individuals to respond to a series of interview questions. Try to find two people who differ in terms of background or the social categories above.

Check for time constraints. Reserve at least 30 minutes for each interview. Conduct the two interviews separately.

Obtain informed consent. Explain the purpose of the interview (to explore early childhood influences on intergroup attitudes) and be sure that each respondent understands that his or her responses may be discussed in class or included in a written report.

Assure and maintain confidentiality. Be sure you tell each respondent that you will not in any way attach his or her name to the responses in reporting or discussing the responses to the interview. It is critical that you maintain this confidentiality in order to conduct the interview in an ethical manner.

Conduct the interview. Ask the interview questions in the order in which they appear in this activity. Be sure to take notes in the space provided or on a separate sheet.

Summarize the interview data for each respondent and then complete the reactions section of this activity.

Provide feedback to the respondents if appropriate. If you have some general conclusions about the early childhood experiences and intergroup attitudes based on discussing or analyzing the interview data with your class you might convey these conclusions to your respondents. Be sure to thank them for the time spent assisting you with this activity.

Participant A

Read to respondent: Each of the following questions will ask you about early childhood messages about people who are different from you. As you answer these questions you may focus on whatever social categories (such as race, ethnicity, religion, or gender) are most relevant to your experience.

Interview questions:
1. To what extent were the families in your neighborhood the same or different from your own family?

2. To what extent were the children in your class the same or different from you?

3. Tell me about the images of people who were different from you that you saw in movies or on television when you were a child?

4. What do you remember about the experiences you had as a child with people of backgrounds different from your own?

5. What statements were made by parents or family members about people unlike yourself?

6. Do you remember hearing any jokes about people different from yourself?

7. To what extent did you have childhood friends who differed from you in terms of social categories?

8. What do you remember learning in school texts or other books about people who were different from you?

9. What do you think was the most powerful childhood influence on your attitudes about people who differed from you in terms of social categories?

10. To what extent do you think these childhood experiences have had an affect on your current attitudes about people in different social categories?

Summary of findings:

Participant B

Read to respondent: Each of the following questions will ask you about early childhood messages about people who are different from you. As you answer these questions you may focus on whatever social categories (such as race, ethnicity, religion, or gender) are most relevant to your experience.

Interview questions:

1. To what extent were the families in your neighborhood the same or different from your own family?

2. To what extent were the children in your class the same or different from you?

3. Tell me about the images of people who were different from you that you saw in movies or on television when you were a child?

4. What do you remember about the experiences you had as a child with people of backgrounds different from your own?

5. What statements were made by parents or family members about people unlike yourself?

6. Do you remember hearing any jokes about people different from yourself?

7. To what extent did you have childhood friends who differed from you in terms of social categories?

8. What do you remember learning in school texts or other books about people who were different from you?

9. What do you think was the most powerful childhood influence on your attitudes about people who differed from you in terms of social categories?

10. To what extent do you think these childhood experiences have had an affect on your current attitudes about people in different social categories?

Summary of findings:

Reactions:

1. Discuss the primary influences on intergroup attitudes of your respondents. If you noticed any differences between the two respondents in the relative importance of these influences, please discuss these as well.

2. To what do you attribute the power of the more influential factors you describe above?

3. Based on your interview data, what recommendations can you make about potential strategies for prejudice reduction?

Reference:

Rohan, M. J., & Zanna, M. P. (1996). Value transmission in families. In C. Seligman, J. M. Olson, M.P. Zanna (Eds.), *The psychology of value: The Ontario symposium: Vol. 8.* Mahwah, NJ: Erlbaum.

Name _____   Date _____

Activity 8.6
COGNITIVE ASPECTS OF STEREOTYPING

Research in cognitive psychology indicates that stereotyping is in part a result of the way humans process information (see, for example, Hamilton, Stroessner, & Driscoll, 1994). The way we categorize, memorize and explain events is generally adaptive, but under some circumstances can lead us to develop and maintain stereotypes. This activity will demonstrate some of the cognitive processes involved in stereotyping.

Directions: You will need to request the assistance of four volunteers for this activity. Each of the participants will listen to a slightly different description. Read the descriptions below to the participant indicated. The participant should then complete the appropriate questionnaire. You will note that the descriptions vary in terms of the age and gender of the stimulus person. Once you have collected responses from all four participants, answer the reaction questions on the following page.

Read to Participant A: We are asking for volunteers as part of a class project on the processes involved in forming mental imagery. Please listen to the following description and focus on the images that form in response. You will then be asked to complete a brief questionnaire.

Jennifer is 27 years old. She is taking courses at her local community college and working part time. A few years ago she moved from a more urban area to an apartment complex in the suburbs. She lives alone, except for a pet. She is in good health and tries to get some exercise several times a week. She has made friends with one of her neighbors with whom she occasionally cooks a meal. She has several hobbies and enjoys the outdoors.

Read to Participant B: We are asking for volunteers as part of a class project on the processes involved in forming mental imagery. Please listen to the following description and focus on the images that form in response. You will then be asked to complete a brief questionnaire.

Jennifer is 67 years old. She is taking courses at her local community college and working part time. A few years ago she moved from a more urban area to an apartment complex in the suburbs. She lives alone, except for a pet. She is in good health and tries to get some exercise several times a week. She has made friends with one of her neighbors with whom she occasionally cooks a meal. She has several hobbies and enjoys the outdoors.

Read to Participant C: We are asking for volunteers as part of a class project on the processes involved in forming mental imagery. Please listen to the following description and focus on the images that form in response. You will then be asked to complete a brief questionnaire.

Jonathan is 27 years old. He is taking courses at his local community college and working part time. A few years ago he moved from a more urban area to an apartment complex in the suburbs. He lives alone, except for a pet. He is in good health and tries to get some exercise several times a week. He has made friends with one of his neighbors with whom he occasionally cooks a meal. He has several hobbies and enjoys the outdoors.

Read to Participant D: We are asking for volunteers as part of a class project on the processes involved in forming mental imagery. Please listen to the following description and focus on the images that form in response. You will then be asked to complete a brief questionnaire.

Jonathan is 67 years old. He is taking courses at his local community college and working part time. A few years ago he moved from a more urban area to an apartment complex in the suburbs. He lives alone, except for a pet. He is in good health and tries to get some exercise several times a week. He has made friends with one of his neighbors with whom he occasionally cooks a meal. He has several hobbies and enjoys the outdoors.

Participant A

Please think about the person who was just described to you for a moment. In the space below, write down everything you can remember about this person. When you have finished writing down what you remember, please answer the questions on the back of the page.

Based on your image of Jennifer, please answer the following questions. If you do not have enough information to answer a particular question, draw on your image of Jennifer to answer as best you can.

1. How old is Jennifer?

2. What kind of courses was Jennifer taking?

3. What kind of work did Jennifer do?

4. Why did Jennifer move to the suburbs?

5. What kind of pet did she have?

6. How is her health?

7. What kind of exercise does she do?

8. Why does she occasionally cook with her neighbor?

9. What do you think she cooks?

10. What are her hobbies?

11. What does she enjoy doing outdoors?

12. Do you think Jennifer is someone you would enjoy meeting? Why or why not?

Participant B

Please think about the person who was just described to you for a moment. In the space below, write down everything you can remember about this person. When you have finished writing down what you remember, please answer the questions on the back of the page.

Based on your image of Jennifer, please answer the following questions. If you do not have enough information to answer a particular question, draw on your image of Jennifer to answer as best you can.

1. How old is Jennifer?

2. What kind of courses was Jennifer taking?

3. What kind of work did Jennifer do?

4. Why did Jennifer move to the suburbs?

5. What kind of pet did she have?

6. How is her health?

7. What kind of exercise does she do?

8. Why does she occasionally cook with her neighbor?

9. What do you think she cooks?

10. What are her hobbies?

11. What does she enjoy doing outdoors?

12. Do you think Jennifer is someone you would enjoy meeting? Why or why not?

Participant C

Please think about the person who was just described to you for a moment. In the space below, write down everything you can remember about this person. When you have finished writing down what you remember, please answer the questions on the back of the page.

Based on your image of Jonathan, please answer the following questions. If you do not have enough information to answer a particular question, draw on your image of Jonathan to answer as best you can.

1. How old is Jonathan?

2. What kind of courses was Jonathan taking?

3. What kind of work did Jonathan do?

4. Why did Jonathan move to the suburbs?

5. What kind of pet did he have?

6. How is his health?

7. What kind of exercise does he do?

8. Why does he occasionally cook with his neighbor?

9. What do you think he cooks?

10. What are his hobbies?

11. What does he enjoy doing outdoors?

12. Do you think Jonathan is someone you would enjoy meeting? Why or why not?

Participant D

Please think about the person who was just described to you for a moment. In the space below, write down everything you can remember about this person. When you have finished writing down what you remember, please answer the questions on the back of the page.

Based on your image of Jonathan, please answer the following questions. If you do not have enough information to answer a particular question, draw on your image of Jonathan to answer as best you can.

1. How old is Jonathan?

2. What kind of courses was Jonathan taking?

3. What kind of work did Jonathan do?

4. Why did Jonathan move to the suburbs?

5. What kind of pet did he have?

6. How is his health?

7. What kind of exercise does he do?

8. Why does he occasionally cook with his neighbor?

9. What do you think he cooks?

10. What are his hobbies?

11. What does he enjoy doing outdoors?

12. Do you think Jonathan is someone you would enjoy meeting? Why or why not?

Reactions:

1. Examine the responses of the four participants. In what ways did the shift in age or gender affect the images generated?

2. Studies of the role of cognition in the stereotyping process generally indicate the following:

- We easily and readily place others into categories.
- We tend to pay attention to and remember information consistent with our stereotype.
- We fill in gaps in memory with information that fits our stereotypes.
- We tend to make judgments about causes of behavior that are stereotype consistent.

Discuss the extent to which the data you collected indicated any of these cognitive processes.

3. Discuss the possible sources of any stereotypes found in your data.

4. Discuss the implications of the existence of such stereotypes.

Reference:

Hamilton, D. L., Stroessner, S. J., & Driscoll, D. M. (1994). Social cognition and the study of stereotyping. In P. G. Devine, D. L. Hamilton, & T. M. Ostrom (Eds.), *Social cognition: Impact on social psychology* (pp. 291-321). New York: Academic Press.

Name _____   Date _____

Activity 8.7
PERSPECTIVES ON PREJUDICE

Psychologist have taken a number of different approaches to understanding issues of prejudice and discrimination. Though different approaches have been emphasized over time, all are currently viewed as making important contributions to our understanding of intergroup attitudes. This activity will provide you with experience using four perspectives to analyze a case of prejudice or discrimination.

Directions: The first task of this activity is to identify a case of prejudice or discrimination. Newspapers, magazine articles, historical documents, and the Internet are all potential sources of such cases (examples include the Rodney King beating, the Vincent Chin murder, and the Sharon Kowalski case). Once you have chosen a specific case, use the descriptions below (categorized under labels from Duckitt, 1992) and in the spaces provided, analyze your case from each of the four theoretical perspectives.

Perspectives:
Prejudiced Personality Perspective. According to this perspective, individual traits such as authoritarianism, dogmatism, cynicism, and belief in a just world make one more susceptible to prejudiced beliefs.

Social Transmission Perspective. This perspective focuses on the messages about various groups that are conveyed to us through family, peers, schools, and the media. The processes of learning (classical, operant, and social learning) and conformity are critical to this approach.

Intergroup Dynamics Perspective. This perspective deals with the conflict that exists between groups who are, or perceive themselves to be, in competition for resources. Associated with this intergroup competition is the tendency to identify strongly with one's own group and to view the outgroup as homogeneous.

Social Cognition Perspective. According to this perspective, prejudice is a result of errors in human information processing rather than a manifestation of an underlying pathology. This perspective recognizes that once we form cognitive categories, we tend to attend to and remember stereotype-consistent information. When relevant information is absent, we tend to fill in the gaps with stereotype-consistent material.

Case Description: In the space provided below, describe your case in detail. Include any information available about the personality, motivation, or life circumstances of the perpetrator(s) and the social context.

Prejudiced Personality Perspective

Social Transmission Perspective

Intergroup Dynamics Perspective

Social Cognition Perspective

Reference:
    Duckitt, J. (1992). Psychology and prejudice: A historical analysis and integrative framework. *American Psychologist, 47,* 1182-1193.

Name _____   Date _____

Activity 8.8
ENEMY IMAGES

This activity seeks commonalities in the way enemies are portrayed and explores the implications of these enemy images.

Directions: For this activity you will need to locate an enemy image. This image can be either a picture or a written depiction of someone viewed as an enemy. Unfortunately, enemy images are not difficult to find. You can find enemy images in wartime propaganda, newspaper editorials, political cartoons, or in the literature of hate groups on the Internet. If possible, make a copy of the enemy image to attach to this write-up and then answer the questions below.

1. Identify the individual or entity portrayed as the enemy.

2. Describe the critical features of the enemy image.

3. Discuss the strategies used to associate the enemy with evil or to make the enemy contemptible to the perceiver.

4. Evaluate the effectiveness of the strategies used to create an enemy image.

Name _____ Date _____

Activity 8.9
THE CONTACT HYPOTHESIS

Many prejudice-reduction techniques are based on the idea that if people from different groups are brought together, they will learn about each other, come to see their commonalities, disconfirm their stereotypes and reduce prejudice. This way of thinking is called the *contact hypothesis*. Unfortunately, studies of contact situations indicate that contact does not always result in decreased prejudice. In fact, sometime contact actually increases prejudice (Monteith, Zuwerink, & Devine, 1994). If people enter into contact situations with well-formed stereotypes, some conditions will further reinforce these stereotypes.

Contact tends to *reduce* prejudice when:

- The contact is between groups that are roughly equal in social, economic, or task-related status.

- People in authority and/or the general social climate are in favor of and promote the contact.

- The contact is intimate and informal enough to allow participants to get to know each other as individuals.

- The contact is pleasant or rewarding.

- The contact involves cooperation and interdependence.

- Superordinate goals are more important than individual goals.

Contact tends to *increase* prejudice when:

- Contact reinforces stereotypes.

- Contact produces competition between groups.

- Contact emphasizes boundaries between groups.

- Contact is unpleasant, involuntary, frustrating or tense.

- Contact is between people of unequal status.

Directions: Read the following scenario and answer the questions below based on the information provided on the contact hypothesis.

Scenario:
Mr. Ruiz teaches a class of 30 students at a high school in Texas. The class consists of equal numbers of students from three ethnic groups: White, Black, and Latino/a. Mr. Ruiz is very concerned about the interethnic relations in his class. There is only minimal interaction between students in the three ethnic groups. In fact, the students self-segregate into different parts of the classroom. When Mr. Ruiz has tried to deliberately assign interethnic pairs to complete a project, these efforts have been met with resistance and, at times, outright hostility.

1. Discuss possible reasons for the intergroup hostility characterizing the high school class described.

2. Describe the steps you would take to reduce prejudice in the high school class described.

Reference:
    Monteith, M. J., Zuwerink, J. R., & Devine, P. G. (1994). Prejudice and prejudice reduction: Classic challenges, contemporary approaches. In P. G. Devine, D. L. Hamilton, & T. M. Ostrom (Eds.), *Social cognition: Impact on social psychology* (pp. 323-345). New York: Academic Press.

Name _____   Date _____

Activity 8.10
RESPONDING TO STEREOTYPES

We have probably all been faced with situations where someone we are speaking with says something based on stereotypes. How should we respond? This exercise will demonstrate, and allow you to practice, a number of strategies for responding to stereotypes.

Directions: Review the strategies described below, then read the scenario that follows and write in your responses to the stereotypes expressed.

1. *Point out alternative explanations for behavior.* Studies show that we tend to make attributions (explanations for behavior) that support our stereotypes.

Stereotype: Those Malaysian students think they are better than everyone else; they only associate with each other.

Response: If I were in another country I might feel more comfortable staying with others from my group.

2. *Explain that individuals who are more visible may be atypical.*

Stereotype: There's Mike, the head of the Gay Student Association. Those people sure look outrageous.

Response: Mike's appearance may be rather unusual, but most gay and lesbian students look no different from anyone else.

3. *Be a cultural interpreter.*

Stereotype: What is it with those people? I try to be nice to them, but they just won't look me in the eye.

Response: I think Ramon and Celia are trying to be nice as well. In Filipino culture, many people think it is rude to have direct eye contact.

4. *Point out within-group differences.*

Stereotype: I'm tired of working with older people. They are so helpless and needy.

Response: Well, maybe Mrs. Burns is like that, but Mr. Santos and Mrs. Ralph are very independent.

5. *Point out similarities across groups.*

Stereotype: Those people play their music so loudly.

Response: Sometimes people get carried away when there's a party. Did you hear the noise coming from our fraternity last night?

6. *Indicate when conclusions are based on limited experience.*

Stereotype: You have to watch Arabs carefully. They could be terrorists.

Response: That sounds like the Arabs on TV action movies. I don't think I have ever really met an Arab. . . have you?

7. *Point out information that does not support the stereotype.*   Studies indicate that we tend to pay attention to and remember information that fits our stereotypes.

Stereotype: Americans are so rich. Tony said he traveled all through Europe before he came to school here.

Response: Yes, but he told us he worked for two summers to save money for that trip.

Scenario: Two first-year students are waiting for the third student with whom they will share rooms. They have just learned that the other student is African American. They are not African American.

Stereotype: Did you hear that our new suite-mate is Black? Wow, it must be something to grow up in the ghetto.

Response:(*Hint*: Be a cultural interpreter.)_____

_____

Stereotype: I bet he's an athlete.

Response:(*Hint*: Indicate when conclusions are based on limited experience). _____

_____

Stereotype: There was one Black guy in my high school who was an amazing athlete!

Response: (*Hint*: Explain that individuals who are more visible may be atypical and/or

point out within-group differences.) _____

_____

Stereotype: He didn't show up for the orientation session. I guess he's not very serious about college.

Response:(*Hint*: Point out alternative explanations for behavior and/or point out

information that does not support the stereotype.) _____

_____

Stereotype: I just hope the three of us can get along. It could be rough.

Response:(*Hint*: Point out similarities across groups.):_____

_____

Chapter 9. Intercultural Interaction

Name _____   Date _____

Activity 9.1
COMMUNICATING HUMOR ACROSS CULTURES

According to Richard Porter and Larry Samovar (1994, p.7), "Intercultural communication occurs whenever a message produced in one culture must be processed in another culture." Such messages include both verbal and nonverbal behavior. Often we deliberately produce messages. Other times we are completely unaware that we are communicating. Members of the same culture frequently share a great many assumptions involved in the process and content of communication. To communicate across cultures, we must not only be aware of the assumptions we are making but also must be able to understand the assumptions of culturally different others. In general, people do not discuss the assumptions involved in communication. William Gudykunst and Young Yun Kim (1997) note that it is often difficult to explain even our own cultural assumptions since they are taken for granted.

Wen-Shu Lee (1994) has analyzed one of the most challenging forms of intercultural communication: conveying humor across cultures. Lee sees humor as a situation in which we must make new conversational rules that involve explicitly discussing the cultural knowledge that we take for granted in the humorous message. She suggests that in a joke the premise on which the humor is based is often unstated. She gives the example of a "Far Side" cartoon entitled "Scientific Meat Market." In this cartoon, "nerdy" looking male scientists wearing lab coats are flirting with equally nerdy female scientists using "pick-up" lines about DNA and cell division. Lee notes two unstated assumptions involved in this cartoon: (1) Scientists are nerdy, and (2) A "meat market" is actually a bar or club where people meet for social or romantic encounters. Lee notes that it would be necessary to explicitly state these premises in order for the joke to be humorous across cultures. Furthermore, in order to translate the joke for members of a different culture, one would have to identify analogous cultural contexts. For example, in the case of the Far Side cartoon described above, one would need to determine (1) what group of people are viewed as nerdy in the target culture, and (2) what place in the target culture enables people to meet in order to have social or romantic encounters. According to Lee, in Taiwan the nerd stereotype is attributed not to scientists, but to the military intelligence officers who determine whether high school students have violated the regulations on hair length. She explains that in Taiwan, a college dancing party may be somewhat analogous to the "meat market" though a bar clearly serves a different function. The purpose of this activity is to consider the procedures involved in communicating humor across cultures as a way to learn about the process of intercultural communication.

Directions: Select a joke you have heard or a printed cartoon from a newspaper or magazine. Then (1) describe the cultural knowledge that is unstated in the humor, and (2) outline the questions you would need to ask of a culturally different individual in order to communicate the humor in the joke or cartoon in his or her culture. If possible, you may take this task a step further and transform the humor in the joke you selected to fit a different cultural context.

1. Write or attach your joke or cartoon in the space provided below.

2. Describe the cultural knowledge that is assumed in the joke or cartoon.

3. List the questions you would need to ask of a culturally different individual in order to identify the analogous cultural contexts.

4. (If possible) obtain the answers to the questions listed in item 3 and transform the original humor to fit a different cultural context. Include the revised joke or cartoon below.

References:

Gudykunst, W. B., & Kim, Y. Y. (1997). *Communicating with strangers: An approach to intercultural communication* (3rd ed.). New York: McGraw-Hill.

Lee, W.-S. (1994). Communication about humor as procedural competence in intercultural encounters. In L. A. Samovar & R. E. Porter (Eds.), *Intercultural communication: A reader* (7th ed., pp. 373-382). Belmont, CA: Wadsworth.

Porter, R. E., & Samovar, L. A. (1994). An introduction to intercultural communication. In L. A. Samovar & R. E. Porter (Eds.), *Intercultural communication: A reader* (7th ed., pp. 4-26). Belmont, CA: Wadsworth.

Name _____ Date _____

Activity 9.2
NONVERBAL COMMUNICATION

Is it possible to be in the same room as another person and not communicate? Even if we do not speak, we communicate through our facial expressions and gestures. Even if we do not move, we communicate through our posture, use of space, and appearance. Nonverbal behaviors serve several functions including repeating, complementing, or accenting a verbal message, contradicting verbal cues, substituting for a verbal message, and regulating the flow of conversation (Ekman & Friesen, 1969). Some aspects of nonverbal behavior appear to be universal. For example, Caroline Keating and E. Gregory Keating (cited in Keating, 1994) found that in a variety of cultures tested, interpersonal distances (called *proxemics*) were closer between people who were acquainted than among strangers. On the other hand, there are also significant cultural differences in nonverbal behavior. Although it may be universal that acquaintances prefer smaller interpersonal distances than strangers, the appropriate distance between acquaintances varies quite dramatically across cultures. According to Edward T. Hall (1966), members of low contact cultures, such as Japan, tend to prefer significantly larger interpersonal distances than Americans and Canadians, who in turn prefer larger interpersonal distances than high contact cultures such as Arabs, Greeks, and Southern Italians. Individuals dealing with someone from a lower contact culture than themselves may feel rejected. Individuals dealing with someone from a higher contact culture than themselves may feel intruded upon.

Often when we think of nonverbal communication, we think of gestures that correspond to specific meanings (called *emblems*). Although the existence of emblems appears to be universal, as any traveler knows there are many cross-cultural differences in meaning. For example, the ring gesture, made by touching one's index finger to one's thumb, is used in different parts of the world with such diverse meanings as okay, a body orifice, zero or nothing, money, and Thursday (Morris, Collett, Marsh, & O'Shaughnessy, 1979). The purpose of this activity is to better understand the function of nonverbal communication and the ways it differs from verbal communication.

Directions: In the space provided below, list all of the words or meanings that you know how to express nonverbally. Then answer the questions that follow.

1. Think about the nonverbal expressions you listed above. How is nonverbal communication similar to verbal communication?

2. How is nonverbal communication different from verbal communication?

3. Do you think the potential for intercultural misunderstanding is greater in verbal or nonverbal communication? Please explain.

4. How would you go about learning the nonverbal behavior of another culture?

5. Look back to your list of nonverbal expressions. In the space provided below, write/draw a dictionary entry for one of these expressions. It may be helpful to refer to a print dictionary for ideas about the format and content of your entry.

References:

Ekman, P. & Friesen, W. (1969). The repertoire of nonverbal behavior: Categories, origins, usage, and coding. *Semiotica, 1*, 49-98.

Hall, E. T. (1966). *The silent language.* Garden City, NY: Doubleday.

Keating, C. F. (1994). World without words: Messages from face and body. In W. J. Lonner, & R. S. Malpass (Eds.), *Psychology and culture* (pp. 175-182). Boston: Allyn & Bacon.

Morris, D., Collett, P., Marsh, P., & O'Shaughnessy, M. (1979), *Gestures.* New York: Stein and Day.

Name _____ Date _____

Activity 9.3
CONFLICT COMMUNICATION STYLE

Much research has demonstrated cultural variability in conflict handling style. This activity will provide you with an indication of how you communicate in conflict situations.

Directions: Using the scale at the top of each page, circle the number that best describes how you feel about each of the following statements. Once you have completed the scale, calculate and plot your scores, and then answer the questions that follow.

STRONGLY DISAGREE 1	DISAGREE 2	DISAGREE SOMEWHAT 3	NEUTRAL 4	AGREE SOMEWHAT 5	AGREE 6	STRONGLY AGREE 7

1. When something I have purchased is found to be defective, I keep it anyway.   1 2 3 4 5 6 7

2. Showing your feelings in a dispute is a sign of weakness.   1 2 3 4 5 6 7

3. I would be embarrassed if neighbors heard me argue with a family member.   1 2 3 4 5 6 7

4. I rarely state my point of view unless I am asked.   1 2 3 4 5 6 7

5. I am drawn to conflict situations.   1 2 3 4 5 6 7

6. If I were upset with a friend I would discuss it with someone else rather than the friend who upset me.   1 2 3 4 5 6 7

7. An argument can be resolved more easily when people express their emotions.   1 2 3 4 5 6 7

8. I would feel uncomfortable arguing with one friend in the presence of other friends.   1 2 3 4 5 6 7

9. In a dispute, I try not to let the other person know what I am thinking.   1 2 3 4 5 6 7

STRONGLY DISAGREE	DISAGREE	DISAGREE SOMEWHAT	NEUTRAL	AGREE SOMEWHAT	AGREE	STRONGLY AGREE
1	2	3	4	5	6	7

10. I like when other people challenge my opinions.　　1 2 3 4 5 6 7

11. After a dispute with a neighbor, I would feel
uncomfortable seeing him or her again even if
the conflict had been resolved.　　1 2 3 4 5 6 7

12. If I become angry it is because I have lost control.　　1 2 3 4 5 6 7

13. I don't mind being involved in an argument in a public
place.　　1 2 3 4 5 6 7

14. In a dispute, I want to know all about the other person's
thoughts and beliefs.　　1 2 3 4 5 6 7

15. I enjoy challenging the opinions of others.　　1 2 3 4 5 6 7

16. When I have a conflict with someone I try to resolve it
by being extra nice to him or her.　　1 2 3 4 5 6 7

17. It shows strength to express emotions openly.　　1 2 3 4 5 6 7

18. I feel uncomfortable seeing others argue in public.　　1 2 3 4 5 6 7

19. There are not many people with whom I feel
comfortable expressing disagreement.　　1 2 3 4 5 6 7

20. I don't mind when others start arguments with me.　　1 2 3 4 5 6 7

21. I feel more comfortable having an argument over the
phone than in person.　　1 2 3 4 5 6 7

22. Getting emotional only makes conflicts worse.　　1 2 3 4 5 6 7

23. I am just as comfortable having an argument in a
public place as in a private place.　　1 2 3 4 5 6 7

24. In a dispute, I am glad when the other person asks me
about my thoughts or opinions.　　1 2 3 4 5 6 7

STRONGLY DISAGREE	DISAGREE	DISAGREE SOMEWHAT	NEUTRAL	AGREE SOMEWHAT	AGREE	STRONGLY AGREE
1	2	3	4	5	6	7

25. I feel upset after an argument.   1 2 3 4 5 6 7

26. I expect a family member to know what is on my mind
without my telling him or her.   1 2 3 4 5 6 7

27. It makes me uncomfortable when other people express
their emotions.   1 2 3 4 5 6 7

28. I am annoyed when someone refuses to discuss a
disagreement with me because there are others
around.   1 2 3 4 5 6 7

29. In a conflict situation I feel comfortable expressing my
thoughts no matter who the others involved are.   1 2 3 4 5 6 7

30. I hate arguments.   1 2 3 4 5 6 7

31. I prefer to express points of disagreement with others
by writing them notes rather than speaking with them
directly.   1 2 3 4 5 6 7

32. It is a waste of time to involve emotions in a dispute.   1 2 3 4 5 6 7

33. I argue in public.   1 2 3 4 5 6 7

34. When involved in a dispute I often become silent.   1 2 3 4 5 6 7

35. I wait to see if a dispute will resolve itself before taking
action.   1 2 3 4 5 6 7

36. If a coworker were interfering with my performance on
the job I would rather speak to him or her directly than
to tell the boss.   1 2 3 4 5 6 7

37. For me, expressing emotions is an important part of
settling disputes.   1 2 3 4 5 6 7

38. I feel uncomfortable when others argue in my
presence.   1 2 3 4 5 6 7

STRONGLY DISAGREE	DISAGREE	DISAGREE SOMEWHAT	NEUTRAL	AGREE SOMEWHAT	AGREE	STRONGLY AGREE
1	2	3	4	5	6	7

39. In a dispute there are many things about myself that I won't discuss.   1 2 3 4 5 6 7

40. Conflicts make relationships interesting.   1 2 3 4 5 6 7

41. If a friend owed me money, I would hint about it before asking directly to be paid.   1 2 3 4 5 6 7

42. In a dispute, I express my emotions openly.   1 2 3 4 5 6 7

43. When I am having a dispute with someone, I don't pay attention to whether others are around.   1 2 3 4 5 6 7

44. In an argument I try to reveal as little as possible about my point of view.   1 2 3 4 5 6 7

45. Arguments don't bother me.   1 2 3 4 5 6 7

46. I prefer to solve disputes through face-to-face discussion.   1 2 3 4 5 6 7

47. I avoid people who express their emotions easily.   1 2 3 4 5 6 7

48. I wouldn't mind if a friend told others about an argument that we had.   1 2 3 4 5 6 7

49. During a dispute I state my opinions openly.   1 2 3 4 5 6 7

50. Arguments can be fun.   1 2 3 4 5 6 7

Scoring: This Conflict Communication Scale is comprised of five subscales. To calculate your subscale scores, first copy your scores from each of the items into the columns on the next page, then reverse the scoring of the items marked with an asterisk (*) so that 1=7, 2=6, 3=5, 4=4, 5=3, 6=2, and 7=1. Finally, sum each item in the column to calculate the subscale score and plot your profile below.

Confrontation		Emotional Expression		Public/Private Behavior		Self-Disclosure		Conflict Approach/ Avoidance	
1*		2*		3*		4*		5	
6*		7		8*		9*		10	
11*		12*		13		14		15	
16*		17		18*		19*		20	
21*		22*		23		24		25*	
26*		27*		28		29		30*	
31*		32*		33		34*		35*	
36		37		38*		39*		40	
41*		42		43		44*		45	
46		47*		48		49		50	
Total		Total		Total		Total		Total	

Reactions: Hall (1976) distinguished between low- and high-context cultures. In low-context cultures, most of what is communicated is done so explicitly. People in low-context cultures are more likely to directly state or indicate what they would like to say. In high-context cultures, the message is communicated more indirectly. For example, suppose you have asked a favor of a coworker and he is unable to offer you assistance. If this had occurred in a low-context culture, the coworker would likely tell you directly that unfortunately he is unable to help. If this same event occurred in a high-context culture, however, the coworker might indicate the same message by giving a vague reply stating that he will do his best to help.

Hall described the United States (most likely referring to the dominant culture of the United States), Germany, and Scandinavia as representative of low-context cultures and placed the cultures of China, Japan, and Korea near the high-context end of the continuum. Latin American, Greek, and Arab cultures have also been categorized as high-context. You may have observed that low-context cultures tend to be more individualistic, whereas high-context cultures are more collectivistic. According to Ting-Toomey (1985) high- and low-context cultures are expected to vary on several dimensions of conflict handling. Low-context cultures tend to be characterized by greater levels of confrontation, public disputing behavior, self-disclosure, emotional expression, and conflict approach.

1. To what extent do your Conflict Communication Scale scores reflect low-context or high-context communication?

2. Differences in conflict communication styles are a common cause of intercultural (and interpersonal) misunderstandings. What strategies would you recommend for resolving conflicts between individuals with opposing styles?

Source:
   Questionnaire items adapted from Goldstein, S. B. (1990). The conflict management inventory: a cross-culturally oriented measure of conflict management style. University of Hawaii Program on Conflict Resolution Working Paper Series, 90-3.

References:
   Hall, E. T. (1976). *Beyond culture*. New York: Doubleday.
   Ting-Toomey, S. (1985). Toward a theory of conflict and culture. In W. Gudykunst, L. Stewart, & S. Ting-Toomey (Eds.), *Communication, culture, and organizational processes*, (pp. 71-86). Beverly Hills, CA: Sage.

Name _____   Date _____

Activity 9.4
Clock Time and Event Time

Robert Levine, social psychologist and author of *A Geography of Time*, suggests that one of the most profound adjustments a sojourner must make is to cultural differences in the pace of life. These differences have also been noted by individuals who move between urban and rural settings, corporate cultures, ethnic groups, and even academic disciplines. The purpose of this activity is to provide you with a better understanding of the role of temporal differences in cross-cultural adjustment.

Levine (1997) reports that a primary distinction in time perception is between *clock time* and *event time*. For cultures that follow clock time, the numbers on the clock signal when to begin and end activities. Cultures on event time, however, focus on the progression of the activity itself to determine when it begins or ends. From the perspective of someone on event time, for example, it would seem bizarre to end an exciting discussion or event simply because you are "out of time." In addition, cultures on clock time tend to use time in a more *monochronic* manner. That is, activities are conducted sequentially; when one activity is completed another is begun. Cultures on event time tend to be more *polychronic*, conducting several tasks simultaneously. Cultures using clock time tend to be far more concerned with punctuality that those on event time.

For example, you may have a 7:00 P.M. appointment to study for an exam with a friend. If you are on clock time, you might arrive at 7:00 P.M., having decided in advance that you will stop studying at 9:00 P.M. since your friend has a club meeting. If a neighbor drops in with some new music he or she might be politely informed that you are studying and can't listen to the music right now. However, if you are on event time, another activity may delay your arrival for the appointment with your friend. In fact, if you arrived at exactly 7:00 your friend might not be there since you are not expected to arrive at the appointed time. On event time you would stop studying when you are finished even if this means that your friend is late for the club meeting. If a neighbor drops in with some new music on event time, you will likely invite him or her in for awhile before you resume studying. In event time, time is much more flexible and less compartmentalized than in clock time.

Directions: First determine whether the culture in which you live is best characterized by clock time or event time. Then spend one day living as best you can according to the opposite time perception. (Most readers of this book will be accustomed to clock time and thus will spend a day using event time.) It may be less stressful to choose a day in which you do not have any classes or life altering time commitments!   Finally, respond to the questions below.

Description: In some detail, explain how you spent your day using a different time orientation.

Reactions:

1. Describe the emotions you experienced using a different time orientation.

2. What values accompany the use of clock time?

3. What values accompany the use of event time?

4. What strategies would you suggest for adapting to a shift in time perception?

Reference: Levine, R. (1997). *A geography of time*. New York: HarperCollins.

Name _____   Date _____

Activity 9.5
ACCULTURATIVE STRESS

Cross-cultural psychologists have used the term *acculturative stress* to describe the strain experienced by individuals who move from one culture to another.   John Berry (1994) has developed a framework for understanding the factors that contribute to acculturative stress. This activity involves the application of Berry's model to your own acculturation experience in order to better understand the phenomenon of acculturative stress.

Directions: Think about an experience you have had acculturating, or adjusting, to another culture. You may have traveled outside of your country or to an unfamiliar region of your own country. Perhaps you have spent time with an ethnic group or social class different from your own. For people entering an unfamiliar academic culture, adjusting to college may even involve acculturation. In the space provided below, describe your acculturation experience. Then review the description of Berry's model and answer the questions that follow in order to analyze your own experience using Berry's approach.

Description of your acculturation experience:

Berry's Framework

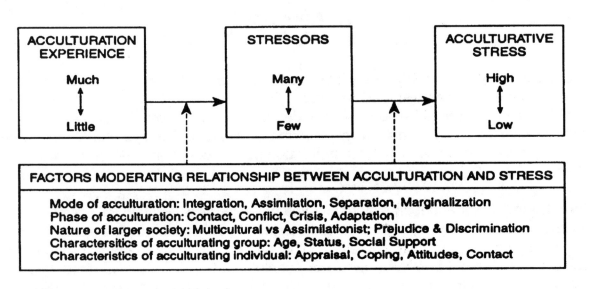

Factors affecting acculturative stress (adapted from Berry, 1994)

According to Berry's framework above, previous experience adjusting to cultural change impacts the degree to which one experiences stressors, which in turn influences acculturative stress. For example, if you have had a great deal of acculturation experience you may be more likely than someone with little experience to view learning new customs as an exciting opportunity rather than a source of stress. Please note that in Berry's framework several additional factors influence the relationships among acculturation experience, stressors, and acculturative stress. These *moderating factors* (listed above) include the mode of acculturation, the phase of acculturation, the nature of the larger society, characteristics of the acculturating group, and characteristics of the acculturating individual.

1. *Acculturation experience*: To what extent were you familiar with the process of adjusting to another culture prior to the experience you described above?

2. *Stressors*: To what extent did you experience stress during acculturation? How do you react to feeling stressed?

Moderating factors

1. *Mode of acculturation*: Berry (1994) describes four modes of acculturation. Which mode, or acculturation strategy, you choose depends on the degree to which you strive to maintain your own cultural distinctiveness (Question 1) and the degree to which you strive to relate to other social groups (Question 2). Research on acculturation seems to indicate that individuals who strive for integration experience the least acculturative stress, followed by those who opt for assimilation and separation strategies. Individuals who choose marginalization strategies, relinquishing ties to their own cultural group while failing to establish contact with other social groups, experience the most acculturative stress. Berry and Sam (1997) suggest further that the acculturation strategy one chooses may vary over time and may be constrained by policies or practices of the culture to which you are adjusting.

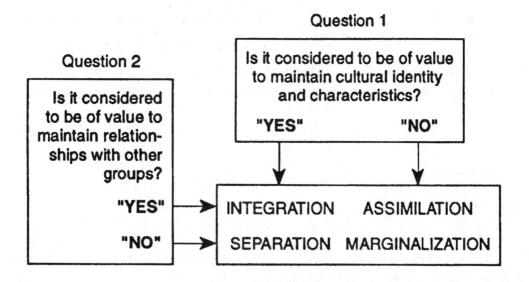

Four modes of acculturation as a function of two issues (adapted from Berry, 1994)

Which of the four modes above best characterizes your acculturation strategy? Please explain.

2. *Phase of acculturation*: Acculturative stress may vary depending on the individual's stage of adjustment. According to the popular U-curve model, stress is lower during the earliest stages of contact, most severe once the "honeymoon" stage has ended, and then decreases again after the adaptation process is well underway. Recent research by Colleen Ward and colleagues (1998) has challenged this idea, suggesting that adjustment difficulties are greatest upon entry and decrease over time. During what stage of the adjustment process did you experience the most acculturative stress?

3. *Nature of larger society*: Was the culture to which you were adjusting welcoming of diversity or was there pressure to conform to cultural norms? Please explain.

4. *Characteristics of acculturating group*: To what extent was your own group valued by the culture to which you were acculturating?

5. *Characteristics of acculturating individual*: What skills, attitudes or personality traits may have increased or decreased your level of acculturative stress?

6. Summarize your conclusions about the factors influencing your level of acculturative stress.

7. Are there any modifications or additions you would recommend for Berry's model? Please explain.

Source:

Figures reprinted from Berry, J. W. Acculturative stress. In W. J. Lonner & R. S. Malpass (Eds.), *Psychology and culture* (pp. 211-215). Copyright (c) 1994 by Allyn & Bacon. Reprinted with permission.

References:

Berry, J. W. (1994). Acculturative stress. In W. J. Lonner & R. S. Malpass (Eds.), *Psychology and culture* (pp. 211-215). Boston: Allyn & Bacon.

Berry, J. W., & Sam, D. L. (1997). Acculturation and adaptation. In J. W. Berry, M. H. Segall, & C. Kagitcibasi (Eds.), *Handbook of cross-cultural psychology: Vol. 2. Basic processes and human development* (2nd ed., pp. 291-326). Boston: Allyn & Bacon.

Ward. C., Okura, Y., Kennedy, A., & Kojima, T. (1998). The U-curve on trial: A longitudinal study of psychological and sociocultural adjustment during cross-cultural transition. *International Journal of Intercultural Relations, 22,* 277-291.

Name _____ Date _____

Activity 9.6
A CULTURE SHOCK INTERVIEW

By conducting an interview with someone who has recently had or is currently having a cross-cultural experience, you will be able to explore the causes, symptoms, and stages of culture shock.

Directions:

Select an interviewee. Find someone who has had or is having a significant cross-cultural experience. It should be someone who has spent at least several months in a culture different from their own. Typically we think of culture shock as something that happens when one travels to another country. However, many other sojourns can result in life changing cross-cultural experiences. For example, when someone raised in a rural area spends time in a big city, when students of color attend a predominantly white institution, or when people travel to different regions of the same country they may experience culture shock.

Check for time constraints. Reserve at least 45 minutes to 1 hour for this interview. Oftentimes people are very excited about having someone to listen to their cross-cultural adventures and they may get a bit carried away with their story telling!

Alter wording if necessary. The questions are worded for the situation in which the sojourn has been completed. If you interview someone who has a sojourn in progress, you may have to alter the wording of the interview questions somewhat.

Obtain informed consent. Explain the purpose of the interview and be sure that the interviewee understands that his or her responses may be discussed in class or included in a written report.

Assure and maintain confidentiality. Be sure you tell your interviewee that you will not in any way attach his or her name to the responses in reporting or discussing the responses to the interview. It is critical that you maintain this confidentiality in order to conduct the interview in an ethical manner.

Conduct the interview. Ask the interview questions in the order in which they appear in this exercise. Be sure to take notes in the space provided or on a separate sheet. Be aware of cultural differences in interview response style. Most psychology research texts suggest that the researcher will lose "objectivity" if he or she enters into a conversation with the interviewee in order to obtain the needed information. However, in many cultures it would seem inappropriate for the interviewer not to disclose information and opinions if he or she wishes the interviewee to do so.

Review and summarize the interview data. Respond to the questions in the reaction section of this activity in order to summarize and apply the interview data.

Provide feedback to the interviewee if appropriate. If you have some general conclusions about culture shock based on discussing or analyzing the interview data with your class you might convey these conclusions to your interviewee. Be sure to thank him or her for the time they spent assisting you with this exercise.

Interview questions:

1. What is your home culture?

2. What is your host culture?

3. What preparation did you receive for your sojourn?

4. How much time did you spend in the host culture?

5. What did you expect the host culture to be like?

6. What was your role in the host culture (for example, international student, tourist, employee, missionary)?

7. How did members of the host culture react to you?

8. What does the term "culture shock" mean to you?

9. Do you think that you experienced culture shock? Why or why not?

10. Please describe any phases of adjustment that you experienced, in other words, did you feel differently about being in the host culture at different times of your sojourn?

11. Did you experience any negative psychological changes such as increased irritability, anxiety, suspiciousness, concern with cleanliness, or hostility toward the host culture?

12. Did you experience any positive psychological changes such as increased confidence, increased self-awareness, or greater openness to new experiences?

13. What was the hardest thing about being in the host culture?

14. What was the best thing about being in the host culture?

15. What was the funniest thing that happened during your sojourn?

16. Was there social support (from friends or relatives) available to you during your sojourn?

17. Did most of your social support come from members of your home culture, members of the host culture, or members of another culture?

18. What new skills did you develop as a result of your sojourn?

19. What was most helpful in your adjustment to the host culture?

20. Can you think of anything that would have made your cross-cultural adjustment process easier?

21. Describe your re-entry into your home culture.

22. How would you compare the difficulty of the original adjustment to the host culture with the difficulty of the readjustment to your home culture?

23. How did others in your home culture respond to you upon your return?

24. What advice would you give to a friend who is about to leave for a cross-cultural sojourn?

Reactions: Use the space provided to answer the following questions.

1. Though we must be very cautious when drawing conclusions based on the responses of a single individual, summarize below what you have learned about the cross-cultural adjustment process.

2. Based on the interview you conducted, develop one research question dealing with cross-cultural adjustment.

3. If you were conducting a study of cross-cultural adjustment, how might you measure "culture shock?"

4. Based on your interview, what recommendations would you make for designing a training session to prepare people for a cross-cultural experience? You can make your recommendations "culture-general" (skills or information that would be useful regardless of the host culture) or "culture-specific" (skills or information that fit a certain cultural context).

Name _____   Date _____

Activity 9.7
INTERCULTURAL COMPETENCE: A SELF-ASSESSMENT

In recent decades, changes in communication, technology, transportation, immigration patterns, and policies of segregation have meant a dramatic increase in intercultural interaction.   However, most of us are unprepared to deal competently with people from cultures that are unfamiliar to us.

A large volume of research has attempted to identify the characteristics of interculturally competent individuals. These studies, conducted primarily with college students and Peace Corps volunteers, have identified several components of intercultural competence. Some of these components have been used to determine the type of person to *select* for an intercultural or international program. Other components have been the focus of programs that *train* people to be more effective in intercultural interaction.

The components listed on the following pages were chosen because they reappear across studies of intercultural competence (such as Dinges & Baldwin, 1996; Hannigan, 1990, Spitzberg, 1989; Wiseman, Hammer, & Nishida, 1989). As suggested by Terence Hannigan (1990), these components are categorized in terms of traits, attitudes, and skills. The purpose of this activity is to provide a means for you to evaluate your own intercultural competence and develop strategies for improving areas in which you indicate a low level of competence.

Directions: Circle the number on each of the scales that follow to indicate your own level of intercultural competence. If you score 4 or below for any of the competence components, use the space provided to the right of the item to plan strategies for increasing your level of intercultural competence. Be creative in planning strategies for improvement. These could include such actions as reading on certain topics, gaining experience in a particular circumstance, rewarding yourself for changing your behavior patterns, or practicing certain skills. Once you have completed the competence component scales and have planned strategies for improvement, please answer the questions that follow.

Competence Component   **Strategy for Improvement**

Traits:

1. Tolerance for ambiguity

   $\overline{}$
   1   2   3   4   5   6   7
   Low   High

2. Empathy

   $\overline{}$
   1   2   3   4   5   6   7
   Low   High

3. Cooperativeness

   $\overline{}$
   1   2   3   4   5   6   7
   Low   High

Attitudes:

1. Motivation to learn about
   cultural differences

   $\overline{}$
   1   2   3   4   5   6   7
   Low   High

2. Respect for culturally different
   beliefs and practices

   $\overline{}$
   1   2   3   4   5   6   7
   Low   High

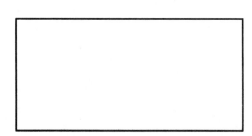

Competence Component   **Strategy for Improvement**

3. Expectation of positive
   intercultural interaction

1	2	3	4	5	6	7
   Low   High

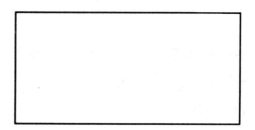

Skills:

1. Ability to manage stress

1	2	3	4	5	6	7
   Low   High

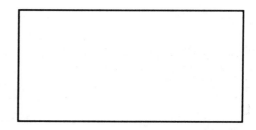

2 Communication and
   listening skills

1	2	3	4	5	6	7
   Low   High

3. Knowledge of cultures that
   differ from your own

1	2	3	4	5	6	7
   Low   High

Reactions:

1. For components on which your scores indicate a high level of competence, please explain the source of these skills, attitudes, or behaviors.

2. Colleen Ward and Weining Chang (1997) proposed an interesting predictor of intercultural adjustment: *cultural fit*. They suggest that researchers examine the degree to which the characteristics of the individual sojourner are compatible with the characteristics of the host culture. Are there cultures for which you might have a particularly high or low degree of cultural fit? (That is, cultures for which you might be particularly well suited or poorly suited). Please explain.

3. Which of the nine competence components might be most readily used as selection criteria? Please explain.

4. Which of the nine competence components might be most readily changed through a training program? Please explain.

References:

Dinges, N. G., & Baldwin, K. D. (1996). Intercultural competence: A research perspective. In D. Landis & R. S. Bhagat (Eds.), *Handbook of intercultural training* (2nd ed., pp.106-123). Thousand Oaks, CA: Sage.

Hannigan, T. P. (1990). Traits, attitudes, and skills that are related to intercultural effectiveness and their implications for cross-cultural training: A review of the literature. *International Journal of Intercultural Relations, 14*, 89-111.

Spitzberg, B. H. (1989). Issues in the development of a theory of interpersonal competence in the intercultural context. *International Journal of Intercultural Relations, 13*, 241-268.

Ward, C., & Chang, W. C. (1997). "Cultural fit": A new perspective on personality and sojourner adjustment. *International Journal of Intercultural Relations, 21*, 525-533.

Wiseman, R. L., Hammer, M. R., & Nishida, H. (1989). Predictors of intercultural competence. *International Journal of Intercultural Relations, 13*, 349-370.

Name _____   Date _____

Activity 9.8
STUDYING INTERCULTURAL COMPETENCE

Until recently, research on intercultural competence has been dominated by studies that used rather unsophisticated research designs and methods (Dinges & Baldwin, 1996). The use of such techniques may be due in part to the difficulty of capturing the complexity of the intercultural adjustment situation. This activity encourages you to think about investigating intercultural competence by developing your own research design.

Directions: Suppose that you have been asked by your university to conduct a study to identify the characteristics of interculturally competent sojourners. The international programs office would like to use the results of your study to better select and train students for international study. Answer the questions below in order to think about how you might design a study of intercultural competence. Assume that students from your school on semester or year long-travel programs will be available to participate in your study.

1. What does it mean to be effective in a culture other than one's own? List several criteria below that could be used to determine intercultural competence.

2. How would you measure the above criteria? For example, would you use an interview format or a questionnaire? In addition, who will evaluate whether the criteria have been met? Should it be a member of the sojourner's culture, a member of the host culture, or the sojourner him- or herself? Please explain the reasons for these decisions.

3. At what point or points during the sojourn would you take measurements of intercultural competence? Please explain the reasons for your decision.

4. What demographic characteristics (such as age, gender, race/ethnicity, social class) of the participants would be important to include as variables in your study? Please explain.

5. What might be some of the limitations of using students as research participants in this study? How might you increase the likelihood that the findings of your study would apply to nonstudent sojourners (such as people on international business assignments)?

6. Look back at the criteria you developed for defining intercultural competence. Do you think these criteria would indicate competence from the perspective of people who are culturally different from yourself? Please explain.

Reference:
    Dinges, N. G., & Baldwin, K. D. (1996). Intercultural competence: A research perspective. In D. Landis & R. S. Bhagat (Eds.), *Handbook of intercultural training* (2nd ed., pp.106-123). Thousand Oaks, CA: Sage.

Name _____   Date _____

Activity 9.9
THE CULTURE ASSIMILATOR

The *culture assimilator* (also called the intercultural sensitizer) is a popular and well researched method of intercultural training. It uses a series of scenarios, or *critical incidents*, that involve some sort of culture clash or misunderstanding to prepare people for interacting effectively with culturally different others. The trainee is asked to read the incident and then select the best one of several attributions (explanations) for the incident. The trainee then receives feedback on the appropriateness of his or her choice. The reasoning behind the culture assimilator is that through repeated exposure to the critical incidents, the trainee will learn to make attributions similar to those made by members of the culture involved (Cushner & Landis, 1996).

Culture assimilators are basically of two types. Culture-specific assimilators address experiences one might have adjusting to a particular culture or setting. For example, Venezuelan business settings (Tolbert & McLean, 1995). Culture-general assimilators, on the other hand, use examples from a wide variety of cultural settings to sensitize trainees to basic dimensions on which intercultural misunderstandings occur. For example, one culture-general assimilator focuses on cultural issues within the context of client-counselor interactions (Leong & Kim, 1991). The purpose of this activity is to explore the culture assimilator method of intercultural training by writing an assimilator item of your own.

Directions: Read the sample assimilator item below. Please note that it consists of a scenario, four possible responses, and rationales for each response. One you have read the sample item, follow the steps outlined to develop your own assimilator item.

Sample Assimilator Item (Tolbert & McLean, 1995)

A U.S. negotiation firm assigned Paul, a top negotiator, to buy raw materials from Venezuela. Paul had been abroad for several years in other Latin American countries, so he knew both formal and street Spanish. During some of the negotiations with the Venezuelan firm, Paul brought the presentation down to an informal level of speech. He noticed that the Venezuelans were listening attentively and seemed to follow the ideas and business plan he presented. He was joking around and talking like "one of the boys" since he was confident about the Latin business atmosphere. The Venezuelans listened politely until the end of the presentation. When Paul was finished, they thanked him and he left.

A week later Paul's manager called him into his office. He began by complimenting Paul on his negotiations record. Paul told him how wonderful the trip to Venezuela was and that he was anxious to hear what had happened. The manager then told Paul that he was about to ask him the same thing -- what had happened? The Venezuelan firm called his company and refused to do business with them in the future. Paul was very upset and had no idea what had happened.

Why did the negotiations between Paul and the Venezuelan firm not produce the results he expected?

Responses:

a. Paul should not have taken the initiative in changing the atmosphere and the relationship with the Venezuelans to an informal level. He should have respected the tone set by the Venezuelans. Because of his actions, he was perceived as condescending.

b. Paul's company made the unfortunate assumption that Paul was qualified to enter the Venezuelan culture successfully because of his prior experience in Latin America. Paul relied too heavily on his presumed understanding of the culture. He assumed that all Latin American countries were the same, and he was too informal for the Venezuelan culture.

c. By dropping to an informal level so quickly, Paul created doubt in the minds of the Venezuelans as to the seriousness of the proposal and his company. In Venezuela, a company's approach is a very important part of maintaining its reputation.

d. The company was not ready to make a decision yet. The Venezuelans needed to call more meetings with Paul and get to know him, perhaps over lunches or dinners. The deal needed to be discussed more.

Rationales:

1. You selected a. When looking at this situation from a U.S. perspective, it is a reasonable response. However, being informal is not necessarily the same as being condescending. While Paul should have respected the tone set by the Venezuelans, there is a more plausible response to this scenario. Please choose again.

2. You selected b. This is a good choice. Some Latin American countries do encourage informal business relationships, but that is not the case in Venezuela. Paul should have explored the Venezuelan norms of business relationships before acting in a more informal manner. It is dangerous to assume commonalities in values, beliefs, and practices within countries that merely share a common language. There is another choice, however, that was preferred by Venezuelans. Please choose again.

3. You selected c. This is the choice chosen most often by Venezuelans. Venezuelans prefer a formal to semiformal work environment and mode of communication. Breaking that norm created doubt in the Venezuelans' minds as to how professional and credible Paul and his company were. In Venezuela, a company's credibility is often determined by its approach to business. The business approach is a very important part of establishing and maintaining one's reputation.

4. You selected d. Perhaps the company may not have been ready to make a decision yet. However, the actual response of the Venezuelans was to threaten not to do business in the future with the company, which is a stronger message than simply saying that they are not ready to make a decision. Such a dramatic response is more indicative of an error of something that he did rather than something that he failed to do. Please choose again.

Procedure for developing your assimilator item:
1. *Choose a culture or social group* that you are familiar with or would like to learn more about.

2. *Choose an issue* that you would like to teach others about through your assimilator item. This issue should involve some type of misunderstanding due to culture, gender, or other social group membership.

3. *Write your scenario* using information gleaned from personal experiences, the experiences of others with intercultural experience, observations you have made about intercultural interactions, or reading you have done about culture and human behavior. Be sure to make revisions to your scenario as needed.

4. *Elicit responses from others* about the issue depicted in your scenario. Be sure to ask people who vary in familiarity with the culture or social group involved.

5. *Select four responses* to use in your assimilator item. Choose one response that provides a culturally accurate explanation for the incident depicted. Choose three additional explanations that, although believable to a cultural outsider, do not adequately explain the incident.

6. *Provide a separate rationale for each response* explaining why it is -- or is not -- the best explanation for the incident.

Your critical incident:

Responses:

Rationales:

Source:
   Venezuela culture assimilator item from Tolbert, A. S., & McLean, G. N. Venezuela culture assimilator for training United States professionals conducting business in Venezuela. *International Journal of Intercultural Relations, 19*, 111-125. Copyright (c) 1995 by Elsevier Science. Reprinted by permission.

References:
   Cushner, K., & Landis, D. (1996). The intercultural sensitizer. In D. Landis & R. S. Bhagat (Eds.), *Handbook of intercultural training* (2nd ed., pp.185-202). Thousand Oaks, CA: Sage.
   Leong, F. T., & Kim, H. H. (1991). Going beyond sensitivity on the road to multiculturalism: Using the Intercultural Sensitizer as a counselor training tool. *Journal of Counseling and Development, 70*(1), 112-118.
   Tolbert, A. S., & McLean, G. N. (1995). Venezuela culture assimilator for training United States professionals conducting business in Venezuela. *International Journal of Intercultural Relations, 19*, 111-125.

Name _____   Date _____

Activity 9.10
A DIVERSITY TRAINING INVESTIGATION

Diversity training is a form of intercultural training that arose in the 1980s in response to increased diversity within the U.S. workplace. Such programs were developed to address sexism, racism, and other forms of intergroup conflict while assisting members of the workforce in viewing diversity as an asset (Paige & Martin, 1996). These programs range from hour-long lectures to ongoing programs involving structural changes in the workplace. A variety of surveys indicate that there has been a dramatic increase over the past decade in the use of diversity training in American organizations (Ferdman & Brody, 1996). A variety of businesses, social organizations, and educational institutions have implemented programs to address issues of multiculturalism. Diversity training programs vary greatly in terms of goals, content, and the method of training. This activity involves investigating the diversity training program of a single organization in order to learn more about this growing form of intercultural training.

Directions:

Identify an organization that has conducted some form of diversity training. The organization you select may be any type of business, government agency, or educational institution. In most organizations it may be best to contact the Human Resources office. In university settings, the office of student life or student affairs may also be involved in diversity training.

Make an appointment to speak with the person in charge of diversity training. It may be possible to conduct this interview over the phone, though it will likely take a minimum of 15 minutes.

Conduct the interview using the interview format included in this activity. Be sure to thank your interviewee for his or her assistance once the interview is completed.

Answer the questions that follow in order to analyze the information that you gathered.

Name and description of organization you selected:

Interview Questions

1. Would you characterize your workforce as *diverse*? Please explain.

2. When did your organization start conducting diversity training?

3. What was the reason that diversity training was implemented?

4. Is the training conducted by someone from within or outside the organization?

5. Who participates in the training? Is participation voluntary or mandatory?

6. Please describe the content of the training program.

7. What do you hope will be accomplished by the diversity training?

Reactions:

Janet Bennett's (1986) framework for reviewing models of intercultural training can be helpful in analyzing the diversity training program you investigated. Bennett's framework addresses the goals, content, and process of the training.

1. Were the goals of the program *cognitive* (focused on changing the way people think), *affective* (focused on changing the way people feel), or *behavioral* (focused on changing the way people act)? Do you think it would be easier to make cognitive, affective, or behavioral changes?

2. Was the content of the program *culture-specific* (addressing the experiences of particular groups, such as women or Latinos) or *culture-general* (addressing basic ways in which groups differ, such as communication style or leadership behaviors)?

3. Was the training process more *intellectual* (based on lectures or written materials) or *experiential* (based on discussion groups, role plays, or simulations)?

Bernardo Ferdman and Sari Einy Brody (1996) have developed a framework for investigating several aspects of diversity training. One component of this model distinguishes between three different motives for conducting diversity training:

- *The moral imperative* -- Training is based on values of equality and inclusiveness as well as an emphasis on recognizing and prizing cultural and other group-based differences among people.

- *Legal and social pressures* -- Training is focused on meeting the requirements of regulations such as equal opportunity employment (EEO) laws or the Americans with Disabilities Act (ADA). Grievances voiced by groups within the workforce may also result in diversity training as the organization becomes concerned with avoiding lawsuits or complaints.

- *Business success and competitiveness* -- Training is based on the belief that the organization will be more productive if diversity is addressed. Diversity training is thus implemented in order to increase the retention of workers, improve communication among members of the workforce, and prepare workers to interact with a diverse clientele.

4. Discuss which of these motives best characterizes the diversity training program you investigated. How will this motivation impact the outcome of the training program?

5. What criteria would you use to determine if a diversity training program has been effective?

6. In the space provided below, please give your overall assessment of the diversity training program you investigated. Do you think it will be effective? Why or why not?

References:

   Bennett, J. M. (1986). Modes of cross-cultural training: Conceptualizing cross-cultural training as education. *International Journal of Intercultural Relations, 10,* 117-134.

   Ferdman, B. H., & Brody, S. E. (1996). Models of diversity training. In D. Landis & R. S. Bhagat (Eds.), *Handbook of intercultural training* (2nd ed., pp. 282-303). Thousand Oaks, CA: Sage.

   Paige, R. M., & Martin, J. N. (1996). Ethics in intercultural training. In D. Landis & R. S. Bhagat (Eds.), *Handbook of intercultural training* (2nd ed., pp. 35-60). Thousand Oaks, CA: Sage.

Answers

1.1 Is Psychology Culture Bound?

Although there is evidence that many psychological finding are universal, cross-cultural research has challenged each of the seven psychological concepts listed in this activity.

1. *Susceptibility to visual illusions* -- A set of classic studies by Marshall Segall, Donald Campbell, and Melville Herskovits (1966) demonstrated cultural differences in susceptibility to certain visual illusions.   Explanations for these findings focused on differences in exposure to (a) angular structures (the "carpentered world theory"), (b) parallel lines extending into the distance (the "front-horizontal foreshortening theory"), and (c) two-dimensional representations of actual objects (the "symbolizing three dimensions in two theory").

2. *The serial position effect (primacy and recency)* -- Studies suggest that the serial position effect may be tied to specific memory strategies developed through formal schooling. Cole and Scribner (1974), for example, found no evidence of a serial position effect in studying memory among the Kpelle people of Liberia.

3. *The independent self* -- Markus and Kitayama (1991) distinguish between independent and interdependent construals of self. Although individualists may focus on the unique qualities that distinguish them from others, the collectivist self is an entity that has little meaning without reference to the group.

4. *Secure attachment* -- Studies indicate a great deal of cultural variability in what is viewed as the ideal form of attachment between children and caregivers. The number of cultures in which stable multiple caregivers are seen as essential for raising well-adjusted children challenges the notion that a secure mother-child relationship is the key to well-being.

5. *Hallucinations* -- Much research indicates that criteria for normality are culture-bound. Although World Health Organization data (WHO, 1979) indicates that visual and auditory hallucinations are found cross-culturally as symptoms of schizophrenia, they are also forms of acceptable behavior in a variety of cultures that sanction altered states of consciousness as part of specific rituals or healing practices (Ward, 1989).

6. *Fundamental attribution error* -- Research in collectivist cultures has generally not supported the fundamental attribution error. Since fundamental attribution error is based on an overestimation of the role of personality factors, it may require a view of the self as independent of the situation (more common in individualistic cultures).

7. *Social loafing* -- Although research in individualist cultures has tended to demonstrate that individual productivity decreases in larger groups, studies in collectivist cultures indicate that being in a group may actually enhance individual performance (see for example, Karau & Williams, 1993).

References:
Cole, M., & Scribner, S. (1974). *Culture and thought: A psychological introduction.* New York: Wiley.
Karau, S. J., & Williams, K. D. (1993). Social loafing: A meta-analytic review of social integration. *Journal of Personality and Social Psychology, 65,* 681-706.
Markus, H., & Kitayama, S. (1991). Culture and self: Implications for cognition, emotion and—motivation. *Psychological Review, 98,* 224-253.
Segall, M. H., Campbell, D. T., & Herskovits, M. J. (1966). *The influence of culture on visual perception.* Indianapolis: Bobbs-Merrill.
Trafimow, D., Triandis, H. C., & Goto, S. (1991). Some tests of the distinction between the private and the collective self. *Journal of Personality and Social Psychology, 60,* 649-655.
Ward, C. (Ed.) (1989). *Altered states of consciousness and mental health: A cross-cultural perspective.* Newbury Park, CA: Sage.
World Health Organization. (1979). *Schizophrenia: An international follow-up study.* New York: Wiley.

Activity 1.9 Exploring the World Village

Of the 1,000 inhabitants:

1. *Men and Women*
   480 are men
   520 are women

2. *Language*
   37 speak Arabic
   86 speak English
   83 speak Hindi
   165 speak Mandarin
   58 speak Russian
   64 speak Spanish

3. *Religion*
   45 are atheists
   62 are Buddhists
   329 are Christians
   132 are Hindus
   3 are Jews
   178 are Moslems
   167 are non-religious
   86 are other religions

4. *Places of Origin*
   124 are Africans
   584 are Asians
   4 are Australians
   95 are Europeans
   84 are Latin Americans
   2 are New Zealanders
   52 are North Americans
   55 are Russians

5. *Age*
   330 are children
   60 are over the age of 65

6. *Daily Life*
   333 have access to clean drinking water
   800 live in substandard housing
   70 own automobiles
   1 owns a computer

7. *Wealth*
   200 people control 75% of the wealth
   200 people receive 2% of the wealth

8. *Education*
   200 cannot read
   10 have a college education

Source:
   Adapted from The World Village Project (www.worldvillage.org)

Activity 3.9 Phonetic Symbolism

English	Mandarin	Czech	Hindi
1. beautiful (b)	mei (b)	osklivost (u)	badsurat (u)
ugly (u)	ch'ou (u)	krasa (b)	khubsurat (b)
2. blunt (b)	k'uai (s)	tupy (b)	tez (s)
sharp (s)	tun (b)	spicaty (s)	gothil (b)
3. bright (b)	liang (b)	tmavy (d)	chamakdar (b)
dark (d)	an (d)	svetly (b)	drundhala (d)
4. fast (f)	man (s)	rychly (f)	tez (f)
slow (s)	k'uai (f)	pomaly (s)	sust (s)
5. hard (h)	kang (h)	mekky (s)	sakht (h)
soft (s)	jou (s)	tvrdy (h)	narm (s)
6. light (l)	chung (h)	tezky (h)	wazani (h)
heavy (h)	ch'ing (l)	lehky (l)	halka (l)
7. warm (w)	nuan (w)	teply (w)	thanda (c)
cool (c)	liang (c)	chladny (c)	garam (w)
8. wide (w)	chai (n)	siroky (w)	chaura (w)
narrow (n)	k'uan (w)	uzky (n)	tang (n)

Activity 6.5 Culture and Mental Health Self-Quiz

1. TRUE. Several core symptoms of schizophrenia and, to a somewhat lesser extent, depression, have been found in a large number of cultures in Africa, Asia, Europe, North America, and South America.

2. TRUE. According to Lin and Kleinman (1988), recovery from schizophrenia in nonindustrialized societies is facilitated by several qualities that are less available to schizophrenics in highly industrialized societies, including support from an extended family, opportunities for meaningful work, and the option to recover at one's own pace.

3. FALSE. Frances M. Culbertson (1997) conducted an international review of the depression literature and reports that although this two to one ratio holds for developed countries, there is no gender difference in depression rates in most developing countries.

4. TRUE. *Karoshi*, death by overwork, is a commonly discussed syndrome in Japan. In fact, Robert Levine (1997) reports that *karoshi* hotline centers have been established throughout Japan to assist workers and their families in dealing with stress-related problems associated with working extremely long hours.

5. FALSE. Lee (1995) reports documentation of anorexia nervosa in several Asian cultures including China, India, Hong Kong, Japan, Malaysia, Singapore, and Taiwan.

6. FALSE. According to Altshuler and colleagues (1988), the reverse is true. Chinese psychiatrists are less likely to hospitalize depressed individuals since a withdrawn person is well tolerated in Chinese society, whereas a manic person is not.

7. TRUE. According to Gerald Russell and colleagues (1996), clients are more likely to be viewed as having a higher level of mental health if they are diagnosed by members of their own ethnic group. These authors suggest that ethnically similar therapists may be better able to understand the behaviors of their clients within the cultural context.

8. FALSE. Expressing depression in terms of feeling "down" is atypical across cultures. Far more common is expressing depression in terms of feelings of emptiness (Shweder, 1985).

9. TRUE. Bond (1991) observes that people in individualist countries, such as the United States and Canada, appear to suffer from more stress-related illnesses than people from such collectivist countries as China, India, and Thailand. This finding may be due to the fact that in collectivist countries there is more shared responsibility for major tasks.

10. FALSE. Cultures differ in terms of whether the most prevalent coping style is active (seeking social support), passive (withdrawing), or internal (thinking through one's own solution). Seiffge-Krenke and Shulman (1990) report, for example, that German adolescents preferred active coping strategies whereas Israeli youth preferred internal strategies.

References:

Altshuler, L. L., Wang, X., QI, H., Hua, Q., Wang, W., & Xia, M. (1988). Who seeks mental health care in China? Diagnoses of Chinese outpatients according to DSM-III-R criteria and the Chinese Classification System. *American Journal of Psychiatry, 145*, 872-875.

Bond, M. (1991). Chinese values and health: A culture level examination. *Psychology and Health, 5*, 137-152.

Culbertson, F. M. (1997). Depression and gender: An international review. *American Psychologist, 52*, 25-31.

Lee, S. (1995). Self-starvation in context: Towards a culturally sensitive understanding of anorexia nervosa. *Social Science and Medicine, 41*, 25-36.

Levine, R. (1997). *A geography of time: The temporal misadventures of a social psychologist*. New York: Basic Books.

Lin, E., & Kleinman, A. (1988). Psychopathology and clinical course of schizophrenia: A cross-cultural perspective. *Schizophrenia Bulletin, 14*, 555-567.

Russell, G. L., Fujino, D. C., Sue, S., Cheung, M.-K., & Snowden, L. R. (1996). The effects of therapist-client ethnic match in the assessment of mental health functioning. *Journal of Cross-Cultural Psychology, 27*, 598-615.

Seiffge-Krenke, I., & Shulman, S. (1990). Coping style in adolescence: A cross-cultural study. *Journal of Cross-Cultural Psychology, 21*, 351-377.

Shweder, R. (1985). Menstrual pollution, soul loss and the comparative study of emotions. In A. Kleinman (Ed.), *Culture and depression* (pp.182-215). Berkeley, CA: University of California Press.

Activity 7.5 Aggression Across Cultures: A Self-Quiz

1. FALSE. Though there have been anthropological accounts of societies with very low levels of aggressive behavior (see, for example, Dentan's 1968 description of the Semai) and societies with very high levels of aggressive behavior (see, for example Chagnon's 1968 description of the Yanomamo) interpersonal aggression is clearly a universal aspect of human behavior .

2. TRUE. For example, Karin Osterman and colleagues (1995) studied forms of aggressive behavior in boys and girls in Finland, Israel, Italy, and Poland. They found that in all four countries, boys were more likely to use verbal and physical aggression than girls. However, girls were more likely than boys to use indirect forms of aggression, such as excluding peers from an ingroup.

3. FALSE. There are societies (such as Japan) with extremely violent media depictions and relatively low rates of violent behavior. There are also societies (such as the United States) with violent media and high rates of violent behavior. Laboratory studies of the effects of violent media (conducted primarily in the United States) indicate that viewers tend to habituate -- or get used to -- violence and judge it as less severe with increase exposure. Studies have been less clear about the link between violent media and violent behavior. In fact, factors such as cultural values and the availability of firearms may *moderate* the influence of violence in the media on aggressive behavior.

4. FALSE. The idea that aggression builds up and, if controlled or repressed, will be expressed in another form, is part of the theory of *catharsis*. Catharsis theory also predicts that levels of aggression should be reduced by engaging in -- or viewing -- certain "acceptable" forms of aggressive behavior, such as contact sports. Research indicates, however, that in the long run, expressing or viewing aggression is likely to lead to further aggression. For example, Canadian and American football, wrestling, and hockey spectators exhibited more hostility after viewing an event than before (Arms, Russell, & Sandilands, 1979).

5. FALSE. Richard K. Lore and Lori A. Schultz (1993) point out that the tradition of a "frontier mentality" isn't always associated with high levels of violence. They explain that among three countries with such traditions, the rate of homicide is very high in the United States, but one third that rate in Australia, and one fourth that rate in Canada.

6. FALSE. According to Marshall Segall, Carol Ember, and Melvin Ember (1997), there is actually a positive correlation between murder rate and number of executions in the United States. That is, the more executions, the higher the murder rate.

7. TRUE. The availability of firearms is a good predictor of homicides in industrialized nations (Morgenstern, 1997).

8. TRUE. Both parental rejection and peer rejection are positively correlated with aggression in children (Pinto, Folkers, & Sines, 1991; Rohner, 1975).

9. FALSE. In fact, according to Richard Nisbett (1996), the reverse is true. People from the southern United States are more likely than people from the northern United States to react to affronts to their dignity with violent behavior. According to Nisbett, this region's history as a herding society has resulted in a "culture of honor" in which such violence restores the social status of the individual or family insulted.

10. TRUE. An association between war and warlike sports has been supported in ethnographic research (Sipes, 1973). This evidence further detracts from the theory of catharsis, which would predict less war in societies with warlike sports.

References:
    Arms, R. L., Russell, G. W., & Sandilands, M. L. (1979). Effects on the hostility of spectators of viewing aggressive sports. *Social Psychology Quarterly, 42*, 275-279.
    Chagnon, N. A. (1968). *Yanomamo: The fierce people*. New York: Holt, Rinehart & Winston.
    Dentan, R. K. (1968). *The Semai: A nonviolent people of Malaya*. New York: Holt, Rinehart & Winston.
    Lore, R. K., & Schultz, L. A. (1993). Control of human aggression: A comparative perspective. *American Psychologist, 48*, 16-25.
    Morgenstern, H. (1997). Gun availability and violent death. *American Journal of Public Health, 87*, 899-901.
    Nisbett, R. E. (1996). *Culture of honor: The psychlogy of violence in the South*. Boulder, CO: Westview.
    Osterman, K., Bjorkquist, K., Lagerspetz, K. M. J., Kaukiainen, A., Landau, S. F., Fraczek, A., & Caprara, G. V. (1998). Cross-cultural evidence of female indirect aggression. *Aggressive Behavior, 24*, 1-8.
    Pinto, A., Folkers, E., & Sines, J. O. (1991). Dimensions of behavior and home environment in school-aged children: India and the United States. *Journal of Cross-Cultural Psychology, 22*, 491-508.
    Rohner, R. P. (1975). *They love me, they love me not: A worldwide study of the effects of parental acceptance and rejection*. New Haven, CT: HRAF.
    Segall, M. H., Ember, C. R., & Ember, M. (1997). Aggression, crime, and warfare. In J. W. Berry, M. H. Segall, & C. Kagitcibasi (Eds). *Handbook of cross-cultural psychology; Vol. 3. Social behavior and applications* (2nd ed., pp. 213-254). Boston: Allyn & Bacon.
    Sipes, R. G. (1973). War, sports, and aggression: An empirical test of two rival theories. *American Anthropologist, 75*, 64-86.

Appendix: Resources on Culture and Psychology

Professional Associations

American Anthropological Association
4350 North Fairfax Drive, Suite 640
Arlington, VA 22204
Tel: (703) 528-1902
www.ameranthassn.org/sctigs.htm

American Psychological Association
750 First Street, NE
Washington, DC 20002
Tel: (202) 336-5500
www.apa.org
   Division   9 -- The Society for the Psychological Study of Social Issues
   Division 35 -- Psychology of Women
   Division 44 -- Society for the Psychological Study of Lesbian, Gay, and Bisexual
          Issues.
   Division 45 -- Society for the Psychological Study of Ethnic Minority Issues
   Division 52 -- Division of International Psychology

American Psychological Society
1010 Vermont Avenue, NW, Suite 1100
Washington, DC 20005-4907
Tel: (202) 783-2077
www.psychologicalscience.org

Asian Association of Social Psychology
(See website for representatives in East Asia, Southeast Asia, South Asia, and the
Insular-Pacific region)
cougar.vut.edu.au/~cynthia/office.html

Australian Psychological Society
1 Grattan Street, Carlton
P.O. Box 126 Carlton South, Victoria 3053
Tel: +61 3 9663 6166
www.psychsociety.com.au

British Psychological Society
St. Andrews House
48 Princess Road East
Leicester, UK
LE1 7DR
Tel: +44 (0) 116 254 9568
www.bps.org.uk

Canadian Psychological Society
151 rue Slater Street, Suite 205
Ottawa, Ontario
K1P 5H3
Tel: 1-888-472-0657
www.cpa.ca

International Association of Cross-Cultural Psychology (IACCP)
(See website for regional representatives in Europe, East Asia, South Asia, Southeast Asia, Insular Pacific, North America, Central and South America, Central and South Africa, North Africa, and the Middle East.)
www.fit.edu/CampusLife/clubs-org/iaccp

Society for Cross-Cultural Research (SCCR)
(See website for current contact.)
www.fit.edu/CampusLife/clubs-org/sccr

The International Society for Intercultural Education, Training, and Research (SIETAR)
www.afs.org/efil/sietar.htm
   SIETAR - Europa
   www.jyu.fi/~sietareu

   SIETAR - Japan
   www.vcom.or.jp/project/international/SIETAR

Society for Disability Studies
Department of Disability and Human Development
University of Illinois at Chicago (MC 626)
1640 W. Roosevelt Road #236
Chicago, IL 60608-6904
(312) 355-0550
www.uic.edu/orgs/sds

Journals
American Indian & Alaska Native Mental Health Research
Asian Journal of Social Psychology
Cross-Cultural Research: The Journal of Comparative Social Science
Cultural Dynamics
Culture, Medicine, & Psychiatry
Disability & Society
European Journal of Intercultural Studies
Hispanic Journal of Behavioral Sciences
International Journal of Intercultural Relations
International Journal of Psychology
Journal of Black Psychology
Journal of Black Studies
Journal of Comparative Family Studies
Journal of Cross-Cultural Gerontology
Journal of Cross-Cultural Psychology
Journal of Cross-Cultural Research
Journal of Homosexuality
Psychology and Developing Societies
Psychology of Women Quarterly
Sex Roles
Transcultural Psychiatry

Anti-Hate Organizations
Anti-Defamation League
823 United Nations Plaza
New York, NY 10017
www.adl.org

Simon Wiesenthal Center
9760 West Pico Boulevard
Los Angeles, CA 90035
www.wiesenthal.com

Southern Poverty Law Center
400 Washington Avenue
Montgomery, AL 36104
www.splcenter.org

Internet Resources

Diversity Database, University of Maryland
An index of "multicultural, multiracial, and multigenerational diversity resources."
Includes directories on age, class, disability, gender, national origin, race and ethnicity,
religion, and sexual orientation as well as a news bureau focusing on diversity-related
news.
http://www.inform.umd.edu/EdRes/Topic/Diversity

Intercultural Communication Resources
American Communication Association Center for Communication Studies
www.americancomm.org/~aca/studies/intercultural.htm

Inter-Links
Resources on diversity related to ethnicity and culture, disability, gender, sexuality, and
religion.
http://alabanza.com/kabacoff/Inter-Links/diversity.html

International Gender Studies Resources, University of California at Berkeley
Includes bibliographies and filmographies on issues concerning women and gender in
Africa, Asia, Latin America, and the Middle East and among minority cultures in North
America and Europe.
http://globetrotter.berkeley.edu/Global/Gender/index.html

Interracial Voice
An electronic publication serving the interracial community.
www.webcom.com/~intvoice/

Resources in Area and Ethnic Studies, New School for Social Research
Includes links to resources on African, African American, Asian and Pacific Rim, Asian
American, European, Latin American, Middle Eastern, Native American, and Russian
cultures.
www.newschool.edu/library/area.html

The Edge: The E-Journal of Intercultural Relations
http://kumo.swcp.com/biz/theedge/
This online journal publishes material with an intercultural theme, including teaching
resources, academic papers, essays, biographical stories, travel stories, book reviews,
poetry, drawings, and photographs.

Web of Culture
A source for information and resources on cross-cultural communication.
www.webofculture.com

World Area Studies Internet Resources, Western Connecticut State University
Includes links to area studies on Africa, Asia, the Caribbean, Europe, Latin America,
the Mediterranean, the Middle East, North America, the Pacific and Australia, and
Russia.
www.wcsu.ctstateu.edu/socialsci/area.html

Graduate Programs in Culture and Psychology
See *International Association of Cross-Cultural Psychology (IACCP)*
www.fit.edu/CampusLife/clubs-org/iaccp